LET YOUR LIGHT SHINE

Becoming the **Best Version** of Yourself

A Woman's Guide to Achieving Personal and Professional Success

DR. STEM SITHEMBILE MAHLATINI

LET YOUR LIGHT SHINE

Becoming the **Best Version** of Yourself

Copyright © 2022 Dr. Stem Sithembile Mahlatini.
All rights reserved.

ISBN 979-8-9864291-9-9

All rights reserved.
No part of this publication may be reproduced, stored in a retrieval system, or transmitted in any way by any means – electronic, mechanical, photocopy, recording, or otherwise – without the prior permissions of the copyright holder, except by reviewer who may quote brief passages in a review to be printed in magazine newspaper or by radio / TV announcement, as provided by USA copyright law. The author and the publisher will not be held responsible for any errors within the manuscript. All characters appearing in this work are _fictitious. Any resemblance to real persons, living or dead is purely coincidental.

Written by: Dr. Stem Sithembile Mahlatini

drstem14@gmail.com
www.drstemspeaks.com | www.drstemmie.com

Facebook: DrStem Mahlatini
Twitter: DrStemahlatini
LinkedIn: Drstem Mahlatini
Skype: Dr.Mahlatini

Foreword by: Dr.Stem Sithembile Mahlatini
Cover Design by: Simba Mukundinashe.

Category: Category: Motivational, Inspirational, Empowerment, Educational and Empowerment

Printed in the USA

Introduction

On Oct 24, 2018, I conjured the courage to go bald. Yes, I cut all my hair and decided to be Free and Fearless. A lot of people asked why?

Some wondered why, but I knew that this bald move was unexplainable.

However, I know why. I was tired of just talking and not moving my life and my work to the next level. I was tired of emotional holds, excuses, unexplained fears, and family values. I was tired!

I also had looked at the calendar and realized we only had two months to the end of 2018, and that was not settling well with me. I needed to promise myself that 2019 was not going to be another stagnant year filled with empty promises, wishes, and a bucket full of plans.

Although 2020 brought us all to a halt, stripping us of everything we knew, it was to me also a year of brevity and baldness. I saw many people young and old get out of their comfort zone and reveal strength that they did not even think they had. It was a time to get out of our comfort zones and become bald beyond our fears, values and beliefs.

Being bald has brought me to another level of baldness. I will now take even bigger risks and take my life to a level higher than I've ever dreamt. I now know being bald means change. Change is not easy. It is true you cannot expect to get different results being in the same place, doing the same things. You will have to change to get different results.

It isn't easy to make changes, but there's no better advice than this: **just do your best.**

Make sure you stay strong enough to move ahead, because there are some wonderful rewards waiting for you when you get the courage to be bald. Not every change you will make will makes sense right away, but with time, you will definitely start to see answers, decisions will prove to be the right ones, and the path will become clearer.

Giving up has never been an option for me. I always tell people that my biggest risk was leaving my parents and siblings in Zimbabwe and embarking to the USA in 1986. After that, every other move and risk had to be taken to live the free and fearless life I came to seek.

My dream is to have enough money to go back and help those in Zimbabwe, build schools, hospitals, training schools and help those that want to start businesses or go to college. To do that, I have to have money, and to have money, I have to take even bigger risks.

In my language shona we have this saying, " Shungu dzarwizi". Ask me in my live workshops to explain, because I will be meeting you soon, if you are reading this. We will absolutely meet and talk about your journey and my journey in one of the many workshops, conferences, seminars that God has prepared me for during this ONE LIFETIME of mine, to let my light shine.

I am so excited of the Women Empowerment Conference I started in 2020 titled "Bounce Back Empowerment Conference, which is held on the third Sat of December every year. Learn more on my website www.drstemmie.com

For three years since moving to Orlando, FL, I honestly thought I could never regain my energy, zeal and excitement of becoming the world renounced motivational speaker, workshop presenter, retreat coordinator, television and radio personality I have always wanted to be. But, today, I am digging my dusty dreams out of my own fears, known and unknown.

I am Ready to Let My Light Shine and help you shine yours as well. There is Room for All of Us and More. Are You Ready?

Let me tell you, I am ready, so ready I can't stop smiling and thanking God for this moment. My vivid, complicated, detailed dreams are back. The running dialogue in my head as I live my life has returned, the big dreamer is dreaming big and acting boldly again. And, I must say, it feels really good!

I know that I have the courage to be fearless. Will you follow along? When my confidence wavers, when I start to mumble, will you remind me fear is a measly four-letter word? Enjoy this guide to becoming a free and fearless you.

This book is a sign of my rebirth. It is the result of my new baldness and boldness. It is my way to help you become your best, as well. I know without a shadow of doubt that whatever I have been able to do, you can do it too, and more. I also know that what others have done, I too can do.

To my parents, Benjamin and Idah Mahlatini, thank you for giving me life.

My siblings, nieces and nephews, I can only be and do the best me to lead you. Be your best and everything will work out. To all my supporters, followers and prayer warriors, may God open up doors for you like never before. Be Encouraged and Encouraging.

After reading this book, I look forward to hearing your story and how you were able to boldly make decisions that have changed your life for the better by living fearlessly and free. Email me at drstem14@gmail.com If you would like me to interview you on my radio show The DrStem Show Be You Be Free Be Fearless

To be interviewed for my Radio/TV/Podcast Email me at drstemshow@gmail.com

You've Only got three choices in life:

Give Up, Give in or Give it all you've got.

Contents

1. Confronting Your Deepest Fear 10
2. Self-sabotage: Reasons Why Women Sabotage Their Careers, Wealth And Success 34
3. Overcoming Self-sabotage 44
4. Understanding And Overcoming The Imposter Syndrome 60
5. Self-care And Self-love: Setting Boundaries That Work And Reducing Stress 76
6. Triumph Despite Lost Dreams 106
7. Unmasking The Greatness Within 122
8. The Role Of Self-confidence In Personal And Professional Fulfillment 134
9. Walking In Your Purpose Unapologetically 146
10. Becoming Financially Empowered 156
11. Becoming Free And Fearless 170
12. Let Your Light Shine 178
13. Conclusion 182

Appendix: 189

LET YOUR LIGHT SHINE
Becoming the **Best Version** of Yourself

Chapter - 01

CONFRONTING YOUR DEEPEST FEAR

"Don't shove down the negative emotions. Let them be seen, acknowledge them, and the move past it. Success has clues".

This Little Light of Mine Lyrics

This Little Light of Mine Lyrics

1 This little light of mine,
I'm gonna let it shine.
This little light of mine,
I'm gonna let it shine.
This little light of mine,
I'm gonna let it shine,
let it shine, let it shine, oh let it shine.

2 Ev'rywhere I go,
I'm gonna let it shine.
Ev'rywhere I go,
I'm gonna let it shine.
Ev'rywhere I go,
I'm gonna let it shine,
let it shine, let it shine, oh let it shine.

3 Jesus gave it to me,
I'm gonna let it shine.
Jesus gave it to me,
I'm gonna let it shine.
Jesus gave it to me,
I'm gonna let it shine,
let it shine, let it shine, oh let it shine.

If you truly want to let your light shine, you must learn to master your fear, known and unknown. You must be willing to do the work to get to the source of your fear and conquer it, head on. Marianne Williamson tells us that our deepest fear is not being brilliant enough, gorgeous enough, talented enough, or fabulous enough. We minimize ourselves so that others don't feel uncomfortable with how talented and fabulous we really are.

The problem is when we do this, we dim our light more, until it doesn't shine anymore. If this is you, eventually, you find yourself wandering around in the dark trying to find how you can light your candle again.

We all have fears, some of which are deeper than we realize. How many times have you wanted to cook a certain dish but decided you just don't have time when in reality, you're afraid it won't come out right? Maybe you've been holding off on wearing that dress you bought months ago because the right event hasn't come around when in actuality, you're self-conscious about your weight.

What about the business you've been wanting to start but haven't because you're just "too busy", when in reality, you're afraid you don't have what it takes?

Of course, you're busy, but you're also afraid you might fail because the last time you tried something outside of your comfort zone, you didn't get the result you wanted. It's time to let go of your deepest fear—the fear of not being 'good enough', not being worth it, not being ready—and take control of your destiny. You have a destiny, but are you on the right path to your destination? It's about time you found your path and let your light shine so that you also create a path for others.

Start conditioning yourself to overcome fear by first honoring your gifts. We all have gifts that are meant to help make a difference in the lives of others and in our own. That thing that you're skilled at and passionate about—that thing that you look forward to every day—is the thing that gives you purpose.

That thing, whatever it is, gives your purpose, drive, hope, and energy; it is your 'why'. Make a conscious decision to make your purpose more important than your fear. Your purpose should win every time, without question. What were you designed to do? What brings you joy? What keeps you going every day? Does your fear of failure or inadequacy deserve more attention than your purpose itself? **No, of course not.** Your purpose should be held on a pedestal while fear lay underneath your feet.

Don't be selfish with those gifts you have; you have them so that you can be a blessing to other people whose destinies are tied around your loins.

Don't allow fear to get in the way of your blessing and the blessings of others.

Once you decide to put your purpose first, you need to confront the standards that you live by and get the bottom of why. Why do you allow other people to tell you how to live your life? Why do you allow other people to tell you that you're not good enough, you're too fat, too aggressive, so on, and so on?

The truth is the majority of us are simply living the lives that society has built for us. We have so easily conformed to the manner of negative thinking that we no longer see things for what they are. You should never allow society or others around you to dictate what your life should be. When you do this, you set yourself up for failure. This is because it's impossible for anyone to determine what your life should be other than your creator.

God knows exactly who you are and what he has in store for your life. He blesses us with people to help guide us and provide counsel, but no one else can dictate or predict what your life will be. God will give you the desires of your heart. The question is, where is your heart and who is conditioning it? Is it you and God, or everyone else?

You have a destiny, and your destiny is in your hands. You get to do and undo it, and whether you win or lose, you are the one who bears the brunt of it all, so why let others determine what goes and what doesn't?

You have the authority to make your own choices and live your best life. More importantly, you are adequate enough to live the life of your dreams. To think that you are inadequate is to insinuate that there is another like you, and you are in competition with that being. You are one of a kind, and no one can be you, no matter how much they try. This means you are adequate by design. Competition is with Only You, that is, if you focus your energy and energy to improving who you are today and who you become tomorrow or who you want to be then you are a Winner.

Stop living your life for everyone else's approval and prioritize your own purpose and desires. It's easy not to recognize how unique, gorgeous, talented, and fabulous you are when you're living for others and not yourself. You are a force to be reconned with, not muffled or controlled.

EMBRACING YOURSELF
The process of embracing yourself can be a long haul, I tell you. It is certainly not for the weak at heart. Many women struggle with coming to terms with who they truly are because they're living up to someone else's standards or in the mirage of what of what past experiences have convinced them of about themselves.

It's easy to envision the kind of future you want, but it's even easier to paint yourself to look like another person...sometimes for convenience or maybe even for comfort or safety. Sometimes, we become so wrapped up in where we are in the 'now' that it's hard to even see ourselves in future terms. We speak of the next five or 10 years, but in reality, we are not doing anything to accomplish plans for the future because we haven't really embraced ourselves, what we really want, and what's driving the fear that keeps us stagnant.

Learning to embrace yourself will help you see your present for what it is and begin the change process. If you could give yourself a hug every day, would you? If the answer is yes, the good news is, you can! Embracing your hopes, dreams, and aspirations for what they are is like a giving yourself a hug on the inside. You are acknowledging that you are worth what you aspire to do and be. You are acknowledging that you believe in yourself and that you are capable of accomplishing even your wildest of dreams. You are signaling that you love who you are and who you are destined to be.

The art of embracing yourself starts with acknowledging your background and accepting it, regardless of what it may be or what stigma or stereotypes may come along with it. Whether you were born with a silver spoon or no spoon at all, accept it. Examine how your life experiences may have molded your thinking and perception of life. Assess whether your way of thinking serves you well or works against you.

Consider how your background and life experiences can better prepare you for the future you want for yourself. Did you have a happy childhood? Were you raised with high standards and values? Did you feel abandoned or discouraged by those closest to you? Have you overcome adversity? Have you done terrible things in your past which you're not proud of? Embrace it because where you are coming from does not determine where you are going.

What is your story and why does it matter? Take some time to really think about this and how it has shaped where you are today and what you want for your future. When you understand your story and all the things that have helped to make you who you are, you gain a greater appreciation for yourself and all you've been through. Then, you're reminded of just how resilient you are and that you deserve a hug. Who better to give it than you?

Many of us feel that we are at a disadvantage in life because of our background, but the fact remains that this background is what made us into the people we are today. Your background strengthened your skills, opened you up to your weaknesses, and has made you into the definition of who you are.

But it doesn't stop there; your background helps you to become the best possible you well into your future. Whatever negative effects the past might have had on you, leave it all in the past. Every moment you have now is an opportunity for you to change what will now become. If you are going to embrace the future, you have to come to terms with the past and own it.

In embracing who you are, you must also embrace your personality. Your personality consists of all the qualities that make you. All those little details that you sometimes look down on or think are ordinary are the things that make you special, and it will shock you to know that no other person in the world has the same combination of characteristics that you have.

No matter how similar others may be to you, there are certain distinctive factors that differentiate you. This is not a mistake; it is what makes you the unique person you are so that you can accomplish the unique purpose that is distinctively yours.

What good is it then for you to try hiding your unique qualities? To hide the things that make you uniquely you is like putting your purpose on the back shelf. No one truly benefits from it, not even yourself, so who exactly are you trying to please?

It is high time you basked in the light that it has brought to your life. Embracing yourself can be tough, even excruciatingly at times, especially if you're allowing society or your past to tell you who you are, rather than embracing your own story and destiny. Remember, you are in control. No matter what your experiences are and how they have shaped you, you have the power to take control of how you will use them to write your life story.

Every other thing or person in your life is merely a supporting character in your story. You are the lead character and, better still, also the writer. Please do not turn it the other way around.

The more you embrace this concept, the easier it becomes to embrace yourself.

BEATING THE ODDS: CAUSES OF FEAR IN WOMEN

It's important to gain a deeper understanding of what causes fear so that you can overcome it. Women have historically been plagued with fear because of societal expectations and their instinctual nature to nurture those around them. From motherhood to the workplace, women are constantly trying to balance all the things in their life without dropping the ball.

You might find yourself asking, "Am I a good mother? Am I doing a good enough job at work? Am I a good wife? Do I have what it takes to be a wife? Can I fit that dress? Am I maintaining my weight?" The list goes on and on. problems that have plagued women, and we will discuss them here. There are several reasons behind our fear of not being good enough. Here are the most common:

1. **Low self-esteem:** Low self-esteem has been known to reduce the quality of a person's life in any gender, but it has affected women's lives much more than others. Low self-esteem is a major cause of fear in women because of the ill traditions that society has subjected us to. This lack of confidence is more common among women because of the image that society has painted for us.

   We are subjected to demeaning standards like, "women should be seen and not heard" and many others such as that. Also, the qualities in which society has used to determine what makes a good woman or a bad one are some of the most detrimental to self-esteem. We are judged based on our looks, which is one of the shallowest things by which to judge a person. All these negative factors that women have had to endure for decades are the major causes of low self-esteem, which over time has translated to fear.

Though not all women suffer from low self-esteem, most women face challenges with self-esteem well into late adulthood. If you're constantly criticizing yourself, it's a sign that your self-esteem might be challenged. Women who are critical of themselves never seem to feel like they're enough, no matter how hard they try.

Being afraid to try is also evident of low self-esteem. If there's something you've been really wanting to do but you find every excuse not to, it may be a sign that your self-esteem is compromised. What's really happening is, you're afraid that you don't have what it takes to achieve the desired outcome. If you were guaranteed a positive outcome for anything you set out to do in life, you'd do it. However, the minute you begin to feel you're not capable, you stall.

You don't have to be perfect at everything you do, you just have to be committed to it. Don't be afraid to do things less than perfect, as long as you give it your best. This can actually help to boost your self-esteem. Perfectionism is actually a major symptom of low self-esteem. Many women become over-achievers because they depend on a sense of a high sense of achievement and attaining excellence to be considered worthy of respect.

Excellence is something we should all strive for, but not at the expense of driving ourselves into the ground. Remember, the only person you need to impress is you. You are your self-esteem's biggest cheerleader.

Although society is not all to blame for our self-esteem because we have a responsibility to ourselves to take charge of our lives' trajectory, it has contributed to more than 70% of the problems that women face in the area of self-esteem. This is why it's so important that you prioritize your needs and wants, and not be consumed with the world's expectations of you. When you put yourself first and believe that you're worth whatever it is that you're working towards, your self-esteem rises.

2. **Self-doubt:** Many women live in fear because they doubt the amount of potential they carry. Self-doubt, which is a close relative of low self-esteem, is a lack of trust in one's abilities. But once again, it is no surprise that many women do not trust in their capabilities because they've been told all of their lives what they can and cannot do, thus being forced to in the shadow of societal and cultural stereotypes. Women are traditionally taught that they're not strong enough or that they can't be too vocal.

This is a major cause of fear in women. After all, how can they launch into the world when they are not even sure that they have the capacity to land safely?

How do you speak up about an issue at work without coming across as too aggressive? How do you take time to relax at home if you're responsible for maintaining a clean house, even after a long day at work? How do you successful maintain your relationship with your significant other while being the best mother possible?

How could you possibly step out of your comfort zone and do anything you're not familiar with? Not only do women doubt the role that the play in society, they doubt what they are capable of actually doing before they even try doing the things they aspire to do. Many women never attempt to explore the full extent of their capacity because they think that those things are not for them.

Being made to live with a mindset that cages them. Some women are even afraid of the amount of attention they would get from climbing higher on the ladder of success, so it becomes almost impossible for them to even see themselves there and trust their skills.

Self-doubt is a barricade to success and presents a huge overcast so that your light is hidden. If you can envision something, chances are you're capable of achieving it. Otherwise, you wouldn't have the vision in the first place.

3. **Lack of support from others:** Every woman needs a support system for encouragement and to help maintain their self-esteem. Whether this comes from family members, friends, social groups, or a spouse, having someone to depend on and life you up is critical to your personal development. Women who haven't experienced the support they needed from others in the past can sometimes feel that they aren't worthy of being loved and supported.

However, this is false. This is the story that women tell themselves when they're esteem is damaged. The fact is, you are worthy of love and support, those around you didn't have the self-worth required to support you. It's time to start loving yourself. Deem yourself as worthy and be open to the support of those who value you.

If you're surrounded by people who tear you down, treat you with a lack of respect, or dismisses your dreams, you make it impossible for your light to shine because your fear of not being good enough only grows larger. This is why it's so important to surround yourself by people who have your best interest at heart.

This isn't always easy to do, especially if you've been hurt or unsupported by others in the past, but when you let your light shine, you'll attract the light of others.

TIPS FOR OVERCOMING PERSONAL FEARS

Everyone is scared of something. Don't ever think you're on an island by yourself when you're faced with fear. Fear is a natural part of life. They key is how you react to it. Will you let fear overtake you or will you overtake fear?

Remember, fear is what helps us to be cautious in the presence of danger; it alerts us to potential dangers so that we can exercise perseverance. But fear should never cripple you from taking a chance on yourself so that you can live the life you envision. It's up to you to put fear in its place and master the story of your life. Here are some ways that you can do this:

1. **The Story You Tell Yourself Will Shape the Life You Lead:** Stories are very impactful. The best speakers in the world are masterful at crafting and sharing stories. This is because they know that stories give people something to relate to. Stories are easy to envision, and therefore make the concepts associated with the story easier to grasp. Stories are powerful because they command the listeners' attention, create a picture in the minds, and influence their perception and behavior.

The same is true for the stories that you tell yourself. Are you telling yourself that you can or can't do something? Are you telling yourself that you will or won't? Is the story you're telling yourself influencing you positively or negatively?

Take some time to think about the story you tell yourself when you're faced with challenges or want to try something new and consider whether you've convinced yourself of possibilities or doom. Then, examine why you've developed the story you've been telling yourself. It is because of something you've heard or seen? Is it because you need to elevate your self-esteem? Is it because you've convinced yourself that the light you once had can't be relit?

Review your story and pick up a red pen. Correct the things about the story you've created that are hindering you. Your story should be filled with positivity and hope, not doubt and despair. It should be something that you aspire to, not dread. The story that you tell yourself should motivate you to lead a life of meaning and break barriers—to live freely and fearlessly.

Telling yourself the right story can completely change your life trajectory because it will create a vision for you to aspire to and motivate you to go get where you want to be in life. The image of yourself that you draw in your mind will help you conquer your fear of the unknown.

When you speak negatively about yourself and what you're capable of, you create the wrong picture in your mind, and you become stagnant. The little things we say to ourselves matter because they sum up to be the totality of our lives. If you were to tell the story of your life to someone else, what would you say? If you were to write a book about how you lived and the decisions you've made which brought you to this point, would you be proud?

If your answer is no, it is time for you to take charge of your life and tell yourself the kind of story that would lead you to live a life that you would be proud of. Shape your life by speaking life into yourself.

Use Positive Affirmations:

Our words are powerful. You may have heard that what we say matters. This is because the words that we use are so much deeper than how they appear on the surface. Just as our stories create images in our minds, our words can affirm the things we want to see happen in our lives.

Our words are the most powerful weapons we have as human beings; they can heal and destroy. They can promote positive thinking or self-doubt and can determine whether we succeed or fail. Our words influence how we think, what we perceive, how we feel about ourselves, and ultimately, influence or actions.

When we speak positively to ourselves, we release ourselves from the hold of fear, anxiety, worry, and negativity of all kinds. There is no better way to change your life than to affirm what you want to see in it through your words. Just as the saying, "you are what you eat", you are also what you say.

When you continually declare the right things in your life, they begin to change your thought pattern. And when you change the way you think, you change your behavior. You begin taking bold action to achieve the vision you've established. You put fear aside and begin to see opportunities in things that you might have considered obstacles before.

Tell yourself that you're worth it, you can do anything, you're a force to be reconned with, you're unstoppable, and that your life has meaning. Wake up in the morning with positive affirmations and remind yourself of them before you go to bed at night. Write them down, say them aloud, and proclaim them to others around you. When you live and breathe positivity, your light brightens the path of your destiny.

2. **Develop your self-motivation:** Self-motivation is necessary to sustain a positive mindset and is critical to perseverance. A positive mindset gives you the energy you need to keep going. Self-motivation helps you to recharge so that you don't run low on the energy you need. Self-motivation is, as the term implies, motivation that is driven by you. This means that you are responsible for recharging your own energy, no one else.

If you're waiting for someone else to motivate you, you're in for a huge disappointment because no one can motivate you like you can. Depending on other people to motivate you to move forward with your life will only you back. No one knows more about what you need to keep going than you do. Everything you need to sustain a positive mindset and commit to your life goal is within you. It's up to you to shine your own light so that you light your own path.

Don't wait for anyone to motivate you, motivate yourself. Focus on what you want and what it achieving it means to you, then remind yourself that you are capable and do your due diligence to achieve what you're after. Be your own motivation so that when others are consumed with their own problems, you will be enough for yourself.

Motivating yourself builds your level of perseverance. The better you become at self-motivation, the easier it is to keep charging ahead when obstacles come your way. Again, remind yourself of why you're working toward your life goal and that achieving it depends on your ability to stay the course. Celebrate your achievements, big and small. Do things you enjoy. Laugh more. Find the silver lining in things, rather than complaining about what went wrong. Focus on what can be if you keep going. Self-motivation will take you far.

3. **Pursue your Personal Mission and Vision:** It's not enough to have a positive mindset and motivate yourself; you must actively pursue your mission and vision. Taking the necessary steps to achieve what you want is the ultimate feat when overcoming fear. The person what you work to become on the inside must be reflected on the outside. The actions you take to accomplish your vision is evidence of this.

Your personal mission is the thing that you want to achieve in life, the difference you want to make in the world. Your mission should be much bigger than you. If your mission only revolves around you, and nothing else, you increase your chances of failure because it lacks meaning and substance. Identify what you're passionate about—what you love to do? What is it that you put all of your heart and soul into because nothing else matters more? That's your purpose...that's your mission.

The vision that you have for achieving that mission is your masterplan. It should be filled with your unique qualities and abilities. It should include what you want to accomplish and how you want to accomplish it. Your vision is your unique work of art. Only you can paint it. It's up to you to step out into the light, pick up your paint and brush, and get to work.

You only have one life to live. Would you rather have tried to achieve your vision or not have tried at all? If you're afraid of failure, keep in mind that you can never go wrong when you're aiming for higher because, even if you don't achieve your desired result right away, you will be in a better place than where you are now. Pursue your personal mission and vision at all costs. Pursue that story that you want to be able to tell—the legacy you want to leave behind.

4. **Change the Way You Show Up:** When your story changes for the better, so do you. Your mindset and the way you view yourself greatly influences how you show up in the world. There is a strong correlation between our mindset and our actions, lifestyle, moods, and attitudes. You cannot become a new person if your habits remain the same. Your mindset must match your actions and your lifestyle. Your mindset determines everything you do—how you eat, dress, walk, talk, and think.

   Your actions must speak louder than your words, which is why it's important that your mindset, words, and your actions align. What good is it for you to say that you can do something but not act on it? When you don't follow your words with action, you don't progress and your vision never materializes.

   Show up like your vision depends on it. You set yourself up for failure when you show up not half-committed or fearful. You must be bold and all in. When you're fully committed to your vision, your attitude changes—things that one bothered you roll off your shoulders a little easier, you smile more, you approach challenges differently, and welcome more opportunities.

You speak and dress in a way that reflects the best possible you. You begin to work on any part of you that does not suit the part.

Take drastic measures to be a better version of yourself, not matter what others might think around you. Don't dim your light or fade into the background for fear of upsetting or offending someone else. You wouldn't turn your headlights off when driving at night because it made someone else uncomfortable, would you? Don't crash and burn because of what others might think. You are on a mission and you need light to get there. It's up to you to show up ready for the journey.

Shine Your Light: Self-Reflection

Take time to reflect on the following questions:
1. What is your deepest fear?
2. Have you fully embraced who you really are? If not, why?
3. What contributes to your feelings of low self-esteem or self-doubt?
4. What motivates you?
5. What are you passionate about? What drives you?
6. What's your personal mission and vision?
7. Does how you show up in the world support your vision?

LET YOUR LIGHT SHINE
Becoming the **Best Version** of Yourself

Chapter - 02

SELF-SABOTAGE: REASONS WHY WOMEN SABOTAGE THEIR CAREERS, WEALTH AND SUCCESS

"Make your mess your message".

When we are scared of something, we avert it. This is a part of human nature. For example, when we are afraid that someone might judge us, we either consciously or unconsciously avoid them. The same is true for situations that cause us discomfort; we avoid them. But what about achieving success?

Humans wouldn't avoid that, would they?

The answer is, yes. In fact, we do it more than we realize. It's a concept known as self-sabotage. It's when we deliberately obstruct something from happening, even when it's something good in our lives. Women, especially, are notorious for doing this.

Self-sabotage doesn't make sense on the surface, but when fear and self-doubt lurk in our minds, we use it to protective mechanism to ensure that we don't set ourselves up for disappointment. When we engage in self-sabotage, the goal is to remain in control of how we fail because we're convinced that we set ourselves up for worse be worse failure if we have no control at all.

However, this behavior is very counterproductive. The fact is, we create our own barriers to success when we do this. This rings true for our home life, work life, and even in our personal relationships.

Consider the following examples:
1. Avoiding dating because you've been hurt in the past and you're convinced you'll have the same experience in a new relationship.
2. Not studying for promotional exams because you're convinced you won't get the promotion anyway.
3. Not signing up for a class you know you need to take because you're convinced you won't pass it.
4. Deliberately putting yourself down because you don't want to be referred to as over-ambitious.
5. Eating unhealthily because you're convinced you won't lose the weight, anyway.
6. Spending unnecessarily because you're convinced you won't meet your savings goal, anyway.

These are all forms of self-sabotage that can obstruct your career, well-being, wealth, and success.

WHY WOMEN SELF-SABOTAGE

The fear of rejection and failure are the most prominent reasons why women self-sabotage. Most women fear that what they really want will never be realized because they're not good enough; they don't place enough value in themselves. They don't want to experience the hurt or suffering that comes with rejection from the people they admire, so much so, that they'd rather pass on their dream for a sense of false security. Unfortunately, this false sense of security results in greater misery than taking the necessary risks to live freely.

It is easy for self-sabotage to go on unrecognized if it has become habit. It's even easier for self-sabotage to go unnoticed if you've convinced yourself that you don't do it to begin with. Many of us dismiss the idea of self-sabotage because we think it's something drastic. However, self-sabotage isn't necessarily limited to major events, like yelling at your boss at work or emptying your bank account in a day. It can appear minor, but if done habitually, can turn into a disaster over time.

Once you understand what self-sabotage really is, it becomes easier to recognize it and correct the behavior. Self-sabotage is that voice that says, "Don't even bother; if don't do it, then how can you fail?", or "You didn't really want it in the first place". Maybe it's a voice that says, "You know you might not be as good as you think...or they think." As a result, you look at other people who seem to be great at it and you become less motivated, so you sabotage your own efforts by not even trying. Odds are, you would have knocked it out of the park if you had only tried.

You intentionally pass on opportunities that could have potentially resulted in success. Self-sabotage is an unconscious calculation of risk that helps us evaluate what we think we can handle and what we believe we can't. But the truth is, you don't know what you can handle until you have experienced it. You are much stronger than you can imagine, but you must put fear aside and welcome new opportunities in your life.

If you we told beforehand about all the evils we were to encounter in this world, most of us would have turned back at heaven's gate saying, "No, this life isn't for me." But you're here, and you're alive and well. Isn't it good to be alive? Thank about all of life's joys, despite the evils and challenges you've encountered. Make it a practice to embrace your opportunities in the same way. Think about all the success you could achieve and joys you could experience if you put fear aside and welcome new experiences.

If you notice habits of self-sabotage, you should begin working on reversing these habits right away. Here are some key indicators that you might be practicing self-sabotage:

1. **Procrastination:** The number one identifier of self-sabotage is procrastination. Procrastination is the act of delaying things that we need to do until they need urgent attention. You might be wondering

how this has anything to do with self-sabotaging. The entire idea behind is that, even though you have the time to attend to what's important, you intentionally put it off. The question is, why? Instead of getting started on what is important, you tell yourself that you need more information or knowledge regarding the said topic or subject before you proceed.

In essence, you need help. You tell yourself that you need inspiration when all the inspiration you need is on the inside of you. It's easier to blame the lack time for when things go wrong than it is to exert your confidence and put in the effort.

2. **Overplanning:** This is when you put everything in place, but you never even start. You take the time to develop a well thought out plan with everything you need, from start to finish, but you can't muster the courage to fully execute it. If you have all the resources to do so without any external opposition, why not start?

Sometimes, we over-plan to make ourselves feel as though we're making progress on something, even though we don't have the courage to actually see it through.

3. **Constant Self-criticism:** Everyone critiques themselves at some point or another. When you're working on self-growth and striving toward a goal, it's natural to self-critique. However, constant criticism is a form of self-sabotage that is counterproductive to your personal growth because it feeds it promotes a negative mindset.

When you constantly criticize yourself, you're messaging to yourself that you're not enough...not good enough, smart enough, pretty enough, educated enough. You constantly rank yourself lower than others.

Self-criticism is a pattern that can also be projected on to others by perceiving their compliments of you as untrue or undeserving. For example, you don't take compliments well because you're so self-critical that you believe people are fabricating their high regard for you and your efforts. Even when others see potential in you, you can't see it yourself.

If all you do is criticize yourself without ever patting yourself on the back for your efforts, you open the door for self-sabotage. Constant self-criticism is a form of belittling yourself and dismissing your capabilities. Remember, you should be sustaining a positive mindset by practicing positive affirmations and self-motivation, not sowing doubt about your abilities.

4. **People-pleasing:** If you find yourself avoiding conflict with others to the extent that you begin to compromise on your own needs, you begin to self-sabotage for fear that people might not like you or that they might hurt you first. You convince yourself that others might not like it if you speak up or stand up for yourself...heaven forbid if you disagree with them on something, so you do whatever it takes to please them, even if it's at your own expense.

   The truth is no one is forcing you to be something else; you sabotage yourself when you dim your light for the approval of others.

5. **Cynicism:** If you believe that everything people do or say is motivated by self-interest, you are likely a cynic. You think that everyone is out to get you or anything that's good at all is too good to be true. This attitude is characterized by a general distrust of others' motives or a lack of hope.

   You're so certain that it's all going to go wrong, that you'd rather question it than believe in it. You self-sabotage by deciding that something won't work or is too good to be true.

6. **Insecurity:** Insecurity can present itself in many different forms. Some women self-criticize and are overly cynical because they are highly insecure about their abilities. Some women are overly dependent upon others, often referred to as 'needy' or 'clingy', because they're not secure enough in their own capabilities. Some women are overly controlling because they're insecure about whether they actually have control of their lives at all.

Maybe you don't self-criticize but you're always making yourself the butt of the joke or laughing at your own ideas because you don't feel that others will take you seriously. All of these behaviors are exhibited when insecurity is present.

Even worse is when you become so insecure that you feel undeserving of the life you desire. An example of this would be if you found yourself thinking, "Oh, that's not possible for someone like me," or "they're not referring to people like me." If you find yourself doing this, you're guarding yourself out of insecurity and you should devote more time to building your self-esteem.

Surround yourself with people and things that make you feel secure and that boost your confidence. Practice stepping out of your comfort zone so that your feelings of security aren't so easily challenged.

Shine Your Light: Self-Reflection
Take time to reflect on the following questions.

1. What are some examples of your own self-sabotaging behavior(s)?
2. Which self-sabotaging behavior hinders you and why?
3. Are there specific types of situations that lead you to self-sabotage?
4. What about failure and rejection do you fear the most and why?
5. How secure are you in within yourself and your abilities?
6. What specific actions can you take to strengthen your self-esteem and raise your level of security?

LET YOUR LIGHT SHINE

Becoming the **Best Version** of Yourself

Chapter - 03

OVERCOMING SELF-SABOTAGE

"You're a choice away from a new beginning and a commitment away from a new life".

You may think you're protecting yourself, but you only harm yourself when you self-sabotage. When you fail to take risks, you fall victim to mediocrity. But you are more than mediocre. You are fabulous. You are beautifully and wonderfully made.

Perhaps you've been struggling with self-sabotage for most of your life. Or maybe you are only just now realizing that you have self-sabotaging habits after having experienced a major loss or disappointment. Either way, it's important to identify these habits and get to the root of them so that your light shines as bright as possible.

It doesn't make sense not to turn on the light switch for fear that the light bulb might not come on. The light bulb works! You just need the courage to turn on the switch. Building this courage won't happen overnight; it requires actively changing your habits, through practice and commitment.

Here are some steps you can take to overcome the strongholds of self-sabotaging behaviors:

1. **Understand the enemy:** Before you can begin addressing your self-sabotaging habits, you need to understand what triggers them. When you notice you're beginning to self-sabotage, ask yourself why. This might make you uncomfortable at first, but it's necessary to get to the root of the problem.

Examine whether there's a specific insecurity or disappointment you're holding to. If it's fear that's triggering your self-sabotaging habits, determine where the stem fears from and work on mending that specific area in your life.

Don't dismiss signs of self-sabotaging habits. It's easy to excuses the behaviors you exhibit when you're in denial. If you find yourself in denial, ask yourself why. What is it about your habits that you don't want to address. Don't deny yourself of the opportunity to get the root. It will only stifle your growth. Likewise, don't blame yourself for self-sabotaging. You are not the enemy, self-sabotage is.

Understand the game that self-sabotage plays, and no matter how valid an excuse you might come up in your mind, choose to acknowledge your self-sabotaging behaviors and tackle them, head on.

2. **Trace the roots:** Trying to get to the root of self-sabotage is the hardest part. You might be thinking, "I've admitted to having a problem. Why do I now have to go as far as finding out where it came from?" Think of it this way—if you plant a garden and then begin to notice weeds growing among whatever vegetables or fruits you've planted, do you just acknowledge them and deliberately allow them to

continue to grow? No, of course not! You would try to kill those ugly weeds at the root because you value your fruits and vegetables. You've invested lots of time and energy in planting and caring for your garden, and you want them to grow strong and healthy. This is the same attitude you should have about yourself.

When you notice damaging behaviors, you should never dismiss them and allow them to continue to fester. You need to determine the source of problem to ensure your personal growth. Consider self-sabotage to be an infection. If it infects one aspect of your life, it is very likely to spread to the rest.

Getting to the root of self-sabotage requires you to do some soul searching. You must ask yourself what is it that you've encountered in life that has caused you to be insecure or comfortable with living up to your highest potential. Why are you doing more dreaming than living? What have you buried deep down on the inside that perhaps no one else knows but you?

Give yourself permission to go there and work on making yourself whole again...through prayer, meditation, positive affirmation, and even professional counseling, if necessary. It is only by killing the root that you can kill your insecurity and strengthen your garden of self-esteem.

3. **Learn to self-program**: Your brain is a powerful machine. In fact, it's the most powerful machine known to man. Your brain is wired to process what's happening around you and triggers a certain action in response. Just as you can program machines, you can program your brain. You have the ability to program how you think and react.

You can do this by identifying specific situations and actions you'd like to take when you're in that situation, then put them into practice. For instance, if you make it a practice to put a book on your nightstand, then read a few chapters before going to sleep at night, your brain automatically prompts you to pick up the book when you see it at your bedside.

Be intentional about performing the action you identified every time you encounter the situation and commit it as habit. This means, every time you find yourself remembering to take the specified action in a given situation, actually do it! Essentially, you are programming your brain to create new and healthy habits. Eventually, your brain will associate specific situations with the specific action you've developed as routine.

You should also make it a practice to clear the filter in your brain to prevent it from being blocked. You can do this by applying the 5 second rule.

There is a 5 second window that defines your whole life. The 5 second between a moment of inspiration/drive and action. If you think about what you need to do for more than 5 seconds, you move from being in control of what you're thinking to falling back into your negative habits.

When you first have the inspiration or moment of drive, count **5,4,3,2,1 and MOVE!** Whenever you notice a block, remember, 5,4,3,2,1. Interrupt it and replace it.

Find your inner strength: The only person capable of winning a battle against you is you. You need to find the strength in yourself to change your mindset. Start by preparing your heart for a change. Allow your heart to be open to love and joy. Think about what you desire for your life and what you're passionate about. Your inner strength is in your 'why'. Why are you striving for what you want out of life?

Or better still, who are you doing it for? The best answer to this question would be that you're doing it for; not for your children, husband, or loved ones, but for you. Do it because you deserve it. Do it because it is your life, and you ought to make the best of it. Once you decide you're worth what you're after, your light becomes brighter so that those you care about most can see it shine, along with the rest of the world.

Finding your inner strength is a process of discovering your purpose and self-worth. But it doesn't stop there. You must align your heart with the proper mindset. Examine what's in your heart. Is it love? Malice? Hatred? Hurt? Joy? Happiness? Root out the things in your heart that are weighing you down so that you also free up your mind.

Your mind and your heart are connected. This means, whatever affects one affects the other. You must condition your heart and mind, just as you would your body during physical exercise. You can do this by positively affirming yourself, being steadfast in your faith, and learning new things that help you to grow every day.

These are the things that allow you to recharge when you feel weary. Don't be discouraged if you stumble and find yourself exhibiting self-sabotaging habits during your strengthening efforts. Like any other strength conditioning exercise, it takes hard work. But if you stay committed, you will see results. How strong are you? Chances are, you're much stronger than you give yourself credit for. Think about all you've already overcome. Use that same energy to open up your heart and mind to new opportunities and betting on yourself.

This form of strength conditioning whips your heart and mind into shape so that self-sabotage doesn't stand a chance. When you strengthen the connection between your heart and mind, you will soar.

4. **Set goals:** One of the easiest ways to overcome self-sabotage is by setting goals for yourself. Setting goals allows you to be intentional about how you live your life. Everything you do should be with an end goal in mind. Setting goals gives you something to strive for—to look forward to. Setting goals also helps to boost your self-esteem because it allows you to track your efforts and accomplishments as you work towards achieving your vision.

Don't allow the idea of setting goals overwhelm you. Start small and expand upon your goals as you accomplish them.

It's quite simple. Think about the vision you have for your life, then write down milestones you need to accomplish in order to achieve that vision. What do you need to put into action? What specific steps do you need to take? What is the timeframe by which you want to achieve each of these steps? What resources do you need to achieve your goals? Write down your answers to these questions and hold yourself accountable to following up on each of goals you've set for yourself.

Finally, setting goals should be fun. Do whatever you can to make working towards your goals something you look forward to so that it doesn't feel like such a chore. Create a vision board, create motivating stick-it notes, and reward yourself for accomplishing even the smallest feats.

5. **Be ready to fail:** If self-sabotage had a lifeline, the fear of failure would be it. Self-sabotage lives and breathes off of the fear of failure. It is impossible to eliminate self-sabotaging behaviors without conquering your fear of failure.

So, how do you conquer it? You must give yourself permission to fail. That's right; it's ok to fail. Every good thing that comes in life comes at a price, and sometimes success comes with the price of failure.

Fearing failure would only push you even further away from your chances of success because the more you fail, the more you see other avenues for success.

Failure allows you to learn and grow. In fact, you learn more lessons through failure than success. Success doesn't drive you to improve upon your efforts because it proves that you already have what it takes to succeed. But failure pushes you to want to do better. You causes you to question what went wrong and seek to understand how you can do it better the next time.

Failure is a learning process by which you grow and prosper. Those who are successful didn't conjure about the formula to success overnight, they failed many times and perfected the process along the way. Failure can also serve as a great motivator. When we embrace failure, there is a strength that rises in us to want to prove it wrong. You must embrace failure as a challenge, not a reflection of who you are. Change your mindset about failure.

Learn to tune out negative thoughts about failure, including negative comments from those around you. Think about failure as an opportunity for growth—a chance to perfect your formula of success.

Too often, we're taught that failure hurts our self-esteem. However, failure does quite the opposite if you allow yourself to be open to it. Embracing failure makes gives you the courage to take more risks that will get you closer to achieving your vision. When you overcome failure, you're motivated even more to keep going because now you know you have what it takes to press on.

You're no longer scared of the unknown since you have already experienced it. Remember, the more risks you take and the more failure you overcome, the stronger you become both mentally and materially.

When you find yourself afraid of taking a risk, ask yourself, "What is the worst that could happen?" When you've hit rock bottom, the only way from there is up. And when you have survived the worst, not much can baffle you. You become an absolute conqueror.

Failure also makes your success much more worth the while. If you achieved nothing but success all your life, you would have no real way of appreciating it. Overcoming failure results in a sense of excitement, gratitude, and appreciation in way that recharges you and motivates you to continue working on your goals and expand upon your vision.

6. **Be Persistent:** Getting something right once does not make you a professional at doing it, just like getting it wrong on the first try does not make you a failure. In the fight to overcome self-sabotage, we have some wins, and we have some losses. It is much more difficult to discard a habit than to form one, and the process of replacing one habit with another can be just as tedious. But you must commit to the process of overcoming identifying and rooting out your fears to overcome self-sabotage.

   Keep in mind that these habits did not form overnight. In some cases, it may have taken years before the habit was formed. Be patient with yourself by rooting out your fear and taking risks over, and over again.

   Don't allow your frustration with the process to cause you to regress to your old self-sabotaging habits. Like anything else, overcoming self-sabotage takes practice, and practice makes perfect.

   Over time, you will be able to quickly. Identify your triggers and learn what sets you off the right path so that you can autocorrect your behavior. You will become an expert in handling yourself in situations where you feel afraid or insecure. You will master your ability to maintain self-control and exercise positive thoughts. You will find it easier to face hard truths about yourself and stand firm in who you are.

Persistence opens the door for you to learn something new about yourself every day. The more you know yourself, the higher your self-confidence. The higher your self-confidence, the less fearful you become. The less fearful you are, the more risks you take. The more risks you take, the higher your chances of achieving your success.

7. **Never Settle:** Too often we accept our current circumstance because we've convinced ourselves that we don't have what it takes to change. We find ourselves thinking, "There's nothing I can do about it", or "I guess this is good enough", even though we know deep down on the inside that we desire so much more.

The more you sell yourself the story of "good enough", the fewer chapters you'll create in your life's story. Make a conscious decision to change the narrative.

Tell yourself that you deserve more. Believe in yourself. Walk in confidence that you are capable of achieving exactly what it is that you want out of life. The world is yours for the taking! There are no limits. The only thing holding you back is you. Be careful not to limit your thinking because of what you think might not be possible. There is nothing you can't achieve that you set your mind to.

Visualize the kind of life you want to live and don't settle for anything else. This does not mean you need to become a perfectionist; it simply means you won't lower your bar because of self-doubt. Your plans may change, and your vision may shift, but your standards and expectations remain the same. The minute you lower them, you open the door to self-sabotage.

You need to have a clear vision of what you want to accomplish, along with clear expectations for your life. This applies to the job you seek, the roles you take on, the relationships you hold, and how you present yourself to the world. Once you see it, you must live it. Many women have the mentality of waiting to see what life brings, but you are responsible for taking charge of your life. Be clear on what your expectations are and don't settle for anything less.

8. **Get over your fear of rejection:** Th fear of rejection is just as powerful as the fear of failure. When you're afraid of not being accepted, you open

the door for self-sabotage, and you set yourself up for failure. You should never take rejection personally. Instead, you should welcome it as a sign of something that wasn't meant for your life at the moment in time...or ever.

Sometimes, we experience rejection because it's God's way of protecting us or it simply wasn't meant for you. Perhaps it was someone else's blessing. If it's meant for you, it will find you. Consider rejection as God's protection. When you view rejection through this lens, you take it much less personally and you become less afraid of it.

Rejection is just like toning your muscles in the gym. The more you train through it, the easier it gets.

Shine Your Light: Self-Reflection

Take time to answer the following questions.

1. What are your key triggers for self-sabotaging behavior?
2. Are your heart and mind aligned when it comes to what you want out of life?
3. What is it about failing that scares you most? What's the worst that can happen?
4. What goals have you set to help you achieve your vision?
5. How often do you settle for less? In what areas of your life do you do this most and why?

How will you hold yourself accountable for correcting habits of self-sabotage?

LET YOUR LIGHT SHINE
Becoming the **Best Version** of Yourself

Chapter - 04

UNDERSTANDING AND OVERCOMING THE IMPOSTER SYNDROME

"Don't discount what you bring to the table."

The Imposter Syndrome is an inner feeling that you are not as competent as others perceive you to be even, in the face of success. It is a phenomenon that is especially prevalent among women where we convince ourselves that we're not as good as others think we are, even after having achieved numerous successes. If you suffer from the imposter syndrome, you tend to believe that all your achievements are by chance, rather than your own efforts or skill.

This feeling of inadequacy stems from believing that you're not worth the success you actually achieve. Hence, you believe it's not possible that you're responsible for your success because you're not worthy or capable enough. As a result, you convince yourself that you're an 'imposter'—you have people fooled into believing that you're intelligent or talented.

The imposter syndrome can surface in any area of your life. For example, you might convince yourself that a promotion you receive at work is because you've convinced people you're the best for the job, not because you're actually skilled at it. Likewise, if you're skilled at a hobby and someone tells you that you should consider starting a business, you might convince yourself that you've somehow fooled them into thinking that you're good at what you do because you don't think of your work as more than average.

The same is true for the relationships in your life. If you meet a gentleman who genuinely thinks you're an amazing woman, you might think you've convinced him of sort of act because you don't believe that you're half as amazing as he thinks you are.

When battling with the imposter syndrome, you'd rather charge the good things that happen to you as luck or chance than to recognize that you are worthy and capable of achieving success on your own merit. The truth of the matter is, you are a phenomenal woman who is incredibly skilled at what you do.

Let that sink in.

Your success didn't happen by mistake. You haven't fooled anyone into thinking you're special. You are uniquely skilled and talented within your own right. The only person you have fooled by believing that you have everyone else fooled about your intelligence is you.

Your success is what it is today because you've earned it.

ORIGINS OF THE IMPOSTER SYDROME

Research has shown that the imposter syndrome often develops in women very early on and are reinforced by societal roles. The Psychotherapy Theory, Research and

Practice Journal cites observations of women who suffer from imposter syndrome during a longitudinal study of 150 highly successful women. During their observation, they concluded that "imposters" typically fall into one of two groups, with respect to early family history.

In one group are women who have a sibling or close relative who have been designated as the "intelligent" member of the family. Each of the women, on the other hand, has been told directly or indirectly that she is the "sensitive" or socially adept one in the family. Here's an example of how the imposter phenomenon develops among siblings.

When one sibling is deemed more intelligent than the other, indirectly or directly, the implication is that the other sibling can never prove that she is as bright, regardless of what she actually accomplishes intellectually.

Let's take a look at Amanda's story. Amanda lives her life in her sister's shadow because it has always been implied that her sister is the most intelligent. One part of Amanda believes the family myth; another part wants to disprove it. She succeeds at obtaining outstanding grades, academic honors, and high praises from her teachers and feels good about her performance. She hopes her family will acknowledge that she is more than just sensitive or charming.

However, the family seems unimpressed, still attributing greater intelligence to the "bright" sibling whose academic performance is often poorer by comparison. As a result, Amanda finds herself constantly seeking validation for her intellectual competence because she thinks her family may be correct. She secretly doubts her intellect and begins to wonder if she has gained her high marks through sensitivity to teachers' expectations, social skills, and feminine charms. Thus, the imposter phenomenon emerges.

The study concluded that a different family dynamic operates for the second group of women experiencing the imposter phenomenon. The family conveys to the girl that she is superior in every way—intellect, personality, appearance, and talents. In this case, it is implied that there is nothing that she cannot do if she wants to, and she can do it with ease. She is praised for being special and ahead of her time. In other words, she is seen as perfect in her family's eyes.

This was Janet's experience. However, Janet began to have experiences in which she couldn't do any and everything she wanted to with ease. In fact, she had great difficulty in achieving certain things. Yet she felt obligated to fulfill her family's expectations. Because she has always been so indiscriminately praised for everything, she begins to distrust her family's perceptions of her and develop self-doubt.

Even though Janet does outstanding work, she has to study and work hard to do well. Because she's internalized her family's definition of intelligence as "perfection with ease," she jumps to the conclusion that she must be dumb. She knows she's far less than perfect, so she must be an intellectual imposter when she achieves success. At least, this is the narrative tells herself.

Unfortunately, far too many women share similar experiences to that of Amanda and Janet. Beyond familial experiences, women receive the same messages from society—women are not as strong as men, women are not as capable of succeeding in positions of leadership, women are better nurturers than they are strategic thinkers. Because these messages have been installed in us for so long, it's natural that we question our true ability to lead, think for ourselves, and break barriers.

You'll never be able to enjoy your success if you continue to harness the feeling of being a fraud and constantly suspect that you will be discovered as such. Beyond being able to enjoy your success, you hinder yourself from realizing your highest potential when you fall victim to the imposter syndrome because success isn't something you feel you truly deserve. If you shy away from success because you convince yourself that you're a phony, you'll fall into the shadows and your light is dimmed. Why should you feel like a fraud while living your best life?

You are worthy of your success; it's up to you to own it! Owning your success doesn't mean you're boastful or arrogant; it means you're confident in who you are and what you're capable of.

IDENTIFYING IMPOSTER SYNDROME: SIGNS AND HABITS

It's possible that you are plagued by Imposter Syndrome and don't even realize it. Here are a few signs and habits you should be cognizant of when determining whether you suffer from imposter syndrome:

1. **Even the smallest mistake is not permissible:** The majority of women dealing with Imposter Syndrome have one thing in common; if it's not perfect, then it's not acceptable. Why is this? Because they believe that any little mistake or imperfection will cause others to see through the wall that masks their fraud. They believe that the smallest mistake is proof that they are not who they say they are or that they're not as competent as they pose to be.

2. **Everything is attributed to luck:** When was the last time you truly believed your skill and expertise helped you to achieve something? When did you last feel confident in your abilities and believed they were the reason for your success? How often to you attribute your success to luck or chance?

It's true that all things work together for our good, and the God puts the right things and people in our lives at the right time, but, as the saying goes, "heaven helps those who help themselves." Give yourself the credit you deserve for helping yourself along the way.

Stop downplaying your achievements because you don't want to acknowledge how special you are. Have pride in what you do and accept that you play a significant role in your success.

3. **You're defensive when faced with criticism:** Many of us see the inability to take constructive criticism as more of an attribute of pride, but it's actually another effect of Imposter Syndrome. Criticism isn't always designed to hurt us, when delivered constructively, it's actually meant to help us. However, if you suffer from impostor syndrome, everyone's out to hurt you because you don't believe you're good enough to begin with. We've all been there.

Maybe a spouse tells you that you could have seasoned dinner a little more, a co-worker tells you that you should consider elaborating on a report or presentation, a child tells you that you should loosen up a little and be a more fun mom, or a boss tells you that you should speak up more in meetings. When you suffer from imposter syndrome, your response immediate response would be to take offense in an effort to protect your already fragile self-esteem. As a result, you might lose control of your emotions and lash out. Likewise, you might cower under pressure and become tongue-tied.

The danger in not addressing imposter syndrome in situations like these is that others begin to label you as things like, aggressive, having a bad attitude, emotional, timid, or uninvested. The problem is not that you have a bad attitude or that you're uninvested.

The real problem is that your self-esteem doesn't allow you to be open to the idea of self-improvement because you already feel like such a failure.

Many of us have accepted these personality labels as the reason why we act. However, people's labels don't define you, your self-esteem does.

IMPOSTER SYNDROME, PERSONALITY, AND TEMPERAMENT

Another way to identify whether you're exhibiting habits of the imposter syndrome is to pay close attention to your personality and temperament. Women who suffer with imposter syndrome typically fall into one of the following four categories:

1. **The perfectionist:** These are women who can never find satisfaction with their work, no matter how incredible it is. Even if there's nothing wrong with their work or performance, they find something wrong. They pressure themselves to achieve more than they should and are always anxious to find loopholes.

2. **The Hero:** This is characteristic of women who never seem to sleep, or even stay still. They never feel that their current achievements are enough and constantly feel that something is missing, so they compel themselves to work harder. Beyond wanting the be a role model, they overwork to save the world and others like themselves.

3. **The individualist:** These are women who would rather work alone and who tend to have an air of knowing all things. They avoid working with others so that no one recognizes they need help.

4. The genius: These are women who constantly set very high goals and unrealistic expectations for themselves, but are disappointed when they don't achieve them. They never start small and put unnecessary pressure on themselves in terms of what they should know and be able to achieve. An example of this would be a woman who has two PhD's but feels she needs a third, even if her job or field of work doesn't require it for her to succeed.

TIPS FOR OVERCOMING IMPOSTER SYNDROME

Now that you have a better understanding of what imposter syndrome is and what signs to look for, it's incredibly important that you take the necessary steps to overcome it. Here are a few that you set you on the right path:

1. Admit it and talk about it: The first step to overcoming imposter Syndrome is acknowledging that you struggle with it and speak about it to someone else. This can be a spouse or significant other, a trusted friend, mentor, or professional counselor. We tend to underestimate the power of expression.

However, exercising the ability to express yourself is a great way to build your self-esteem. It's a great reminder that you have a voice and reinforces the idea that would you have to say matters. It also reinforces your ability to share meaning with others.

2. Be aware: Imposter Syndrome has become a known factor among women, and many people have begun to create awareness about it. Continue to educate yourself about the symptoms and the triggers and remain mindful of the signs and habits associated with it.

When you fail to be aware of your triggers, thoughts, and actions, you rob yourself of the opportunity to rectify them or autocorrect before they even happen. Only those who do not know are helpless in their times of trouble. Remain diligent and mindful at home, at work, and in your personal relationships.

3. Think positive thoughts: If you can control your thoughts, you've already won half the battle. Anytime you find yourself toeing the line of feeling like an imposter, think about your past successes and all the effort you put in to achieve them. Allow yourself to take it in the positive energy that comes with these thoughts; don't shy away from it. Embrace the feeling of knowing you accomplished something for yourself and celebrate yourself.

Use these positive feelings and thoughts to motivate you and build your self-esteem.

4. **Document the process:** Often, the faintest pen remains sharper than the sharpest brain. As human beings, we are prone to forget hardship quite easily. This is not entirely our fault because it is our mind trying to keep us from unpalatable feelings. This is why we easily forget how much we struggled and labored to get what we have today.

    This is also why some people often say that the rich are insensitive to the needs of the poor. It is because we easily forget what we went through before we got to the point of victory. However, this mindset does not help in trying to fight Imposter Syndrome. In fighting Imposter syndrome, you cannot afford to forget the hard work you put in. The best way to do this is to document the process.

    Documenting our journey helps us remember past hardships and allows us to see a pattern in our successes. It reminds you that if you could do it before, then you can do it again. It allows us to both, appreciate the process and establish a set pattern of operations that continue to benefit us along our journey.

5. **Prepare well:** Fear is the absence of faith, and sometimes this lack of faith is in our own capabilities. Lack of preparation can be a great

source of Imposter Syndrome because we leave too many things to chance. However, when we leave things to chance, with no preparation at all, we develop an unconscious fear of failure because we know we're not prepared. It is important that you are diligent in the things you do, thereby establishing a process or routine.

Though you can't control everything, constantly leaving things up to chance will only result in you creating more doubt for yourself. The more prepared you are, the less you have to wonder, and the less doubtful you become.

Furthermore, time and chance only benefit those who are prepared for it. Opportunity without preparation only leads to failure. Preparation ensures that, even when the opportunity presents itself, you would have prepared yourself for the moment. Even if by chance, you happened to be where you are, you were at least prepared for it. Therefore, you were responsible for your own success in that moment, not chance alone.

6. Accept that you don't have to know it all: Convincing yourself that you have to know everything only allows imposter syndrome to thrive. The truth of the matter is it's impossible for you to be and know all things. That's God's role and his alone. Your role is to stand firm in what you do know and seek to learn and grow so that you accomplish the vision God gave you and allow your light to shine so that others can accomplish their vision, too.

When you convince yourself that you have to know it all, you only set yourself up for disappointment and you feel like more of a fraud. This only hurts your self-esteem. Come to terms with the fact that everything won't always be perfect, and you won't always have the answers to every problem. Stop putting unnecessary pressure on yourself to be the end all, be all. It's ok not to know everything.

Shine Your Light: Self-Reflection

Take time to answer the following questions.

1. Do you credit yourself for your successes or are you more comfortable contributing it to chance? Why?

2. What specific traits do you exhibit of the imposter syndrome?

3. What specific triggers do you have? What specific circumstances provoke it most?

4. Which of the four personality traits commonly associated with imposter syndrome do you relate to most and why?

5. How often do you feel the need to be perfect?

6. Do you tend to feel the need to know everything? If so, why?

LET YOUR LIGHT SHINE
Becoming the **Best Version** of Yourself

Chapter - 05

SELF-CARE AND SELF-LOVE: SETTING BOUNDARIES THAT WORK AND REDUCING STRESS

"I experience fear, but it helps me grow. I experience anxiety, but I focus on self-care. I experience pain but, I choose my purpose".

Achieving success is virtually impossible without self-love and self-care. It's all connected. You have to love yourself to believe that you're worthy of achievement. You have to care for yourself so that you're able to achieve the life that you envision for yourself. You have to set boundaries that allow you to care for yourself in the manner that you should.

So many things in our lives go awry because we don't take the time to nurture ourselves—our spirit, mind, body, and soul. Do you know that if you truly loved yourself, you would stay away from certain things? Do you know that self-love comes with sacrifice? When you say you love a person, it is not an emotion; it's an action.

This same approach is true for loving yourself. If we say we love ourselves, we would take better care of ourselves and avoid toxic people, things, and habits to live longer and healthier lives.

Self-love is defined as acknowledging the right to one's own advantage and happiness. It is putting yourself first and choosing to hold yourself in high esteem and value, regardless of the circumstances. Self-care refers to the actions you take in the endorsement of the love you have for yourself. It is essentially anything you do to express and maintain your physical, mental, and spiritual well-being.

THE DISCIPLINE OF SELF-LOVE AND SELF-CARE

Self-love requires discipline. Many women cringe at the thought of self-discipline because it sounds like hard work or somehow implies that we will have to sacrifice all the things they enjoy. However, with great discipline comes great reward. For example, self-love is not helping yourself to a bowl of ice cream whenever you feel like it or refusing to get out of bed and performing miserably at work because you don't feel like it, nor is it pampering yourself by shopping to the point where you make a mess of your savings.

Self-love is placing enough value on yourself that you are willing to sacrifice certain things to give yourself the best kind of life possible. Furthermore, practicing self-love provides you with the opportunity to do discover yourself and do more of the things you enjoy in a way that advances your growth and brightens your light.

One of the greatest misconceptions about self-love and self-care is that they equate to selfishness. Self-love is often misconstrued to mean taking the opportunity to put your personal needs above all else, even at the expense of others. However, this couldn't be further from the truth. Self-love is the process of loving yourself, in spite of others, not at the expense of others.

It doesn't mean that you dismiss your responsibilities as a wife, mother, working professional, or business owner; it means you ensure that you love and nurture yourself first so that you are your best self at home, at work, and in your relationships.

Just as you would fill your car with gas and check your mirrors before driving it, you should maintain your inner and outer self to ensure that you don't crash and hurt yourself, your business, or those around you. The way we show up in the world and treat others reflects the value that we put on ourselves. Self-love and self-care also translate to giving because it allows us to get to a place where we find joy in ourselves. Once you've found joy within yourself, it's impossible for it to not overflow. The lack of self-love results in selfishness, bitterness, and even hatred.

Self-love and self-care demands that we place higher value on our personal well-being then we do material things. When you decide that saving for your business is more important than having the latest designer purse, you demonstrate self-love. When you decide that the latest designer lipstick doesn't define your beauty, the curves of your lips do, it's a sign of self-love.

Self-love is loving yourself for who you are, unconditionally, no matter what. There's no flaw that should cause you to stop loving yourself, no mistake, no past disappointment, no exceptions. You must learn to love you just because God loved you enough to create you just the way you are. What's not to love about that? How could you not love that you were beautifully and wonderfully made? There's no excuse for you not to love yourself.

Your inner being is waiting on you to say, "I love you too".

PUTTING SELF-LOVE AND SELF-CARE INTO PRACTICE

Take some time to consider how you expect others to treat you for you to feel genuinely loved and cared for. Ideally, they'd respect you, spend time with you, give you undivided attention, value your hopes, dreams, ideas and opinions, protect you, make you feel safe, support you, and do things for you that make you happy. These are all reasonable expectations. However, it's less likely that you'll be open to, or even have the capacity to receive any of these things if you don't provide them for yourself first.

If you really want to receive and be able to give love so that you live every aspect of your life to the fullest, you must make self-love and self-care a priority. This will require you to take the same list of expectations you have of others and apply it to yourself. Here are just a few things you should be doing to practice self-love every day.

1. **Practice self-respect**. Make it a practice not to say or do things that demean or belittle yourself. This means being mindful of how you speak about yourself, how you dress, and how you allow others to treat you.

2. **Spend time with yourself**: Get used to enjoying your own company. If you can't stand being with yourself, how can you expect anyone else to? Get to know yourself by trying new things. Take time to reflect on your own wants and needs. Reflect on who you are and what you want out of life. Make time to reflect on your thoughts and feelings. Eliminate distractions and give yourself undivided attention. Learn to appreciate the time you have with yourself in the same way you'd want someone else to.

3. **Guard your peace**. Protect your energy by controlling with you let into your life. You have full control over your actions, how you spend your time, and who you allow into your life. Make sure that the people and things you surround yourself with lift you up, not weigh you down. Joy equals peace.

4. **Do what makes you happy**: One of the greatest acts of self-love is to do things you enjoy. This might come in the form of relaxation, meditation, participating in your favorite hobby, spending time

with friends and loved ones. Whatever brings you joy and laughter should remain constant in your life.

5. **Be grateful:** Have a grateful heart in all that you do. Appreciate the life you have. When you find yourself tempted to complain about what's not going right or what you don't have, think about all the things that have gone right and how blessed you are to have the people and things in your life that are meaningful to you. Be grateful for even the smallest of things and avoid falling into the trap of comparing what you have to what others have. Remember that what is for you is for you.

   Count your blessings! Whenever you wake up in the morning. Keep a gratitude journal and be specific about what you're grateful for. This nature of gratitude will change your life in that you will begin to see how much you have and focus less on what you don't. This is what makes gratitude good for the soul.

6. **Take pit stops and reflect**. Take time to reflect on how you feel and how your day has impacted your mood. Make it a habit to ask yourself, "How do I feel today?" The last 72 hours have a huge impact on the current day. Feel the day. Don't just crank through the day, take time to *feel* it. It's okay to have one day

off but you have to get back on. Give yourself pit stops throughout the day to give yourself a chance to breathe, reflect, and be grateful. Recharge, regroup, and keep moving forward.

7. **Exercise and practice good nutrition:** Maintaining health your health is a very important part of self-care because it gives you the strength and energy you need to take care of yourself, pursue your vision, and take care of those you love. You'll also live much longer. Two of the best things you can do to maintain your health are exercising and eating well.

Exercising is much more than a means to help you fit into your favorite pair of jeans. It helps you to maintain a healthy weight so that you have more energy to do the things you love. It also helps to increase blood flow and reduce stress. Did you know that the number one cause of death among women is heart disease? The best way to improve heart health is to exercise and eat healthy.

The Centers for Disease Prevention and Control (CDC) recommends adults get 30 minutes of exercise per day, 5 days per week. This can easily be achieved by doing things you enjoy, such as taking a walk for fresh air or bike riding. You can also join online fitness classes or visit the gym with friends. The more you enjoy engaging in exercise, the less it will feel like a chore.

A good exercise routine must be coupled with good nutrition. What you put into your body matters because the foods you eat fuel your strength and energy, as well as support your levels of immunity. This is why it's important to eat foods that are high in nutrients, such as fruits and vegetables, and avoid empty calories found in foods that are high in starch and sugar.

Nutritious foods have endless benefits, such as helping to regulate your digestive system, boosting your body's ability to fight viruses, strengthening your hair, skin and nails, and even helping to regulate your sleep.

In addition to eating the right foods, you should also add plenty of water to you diet. Water helps to purify the body of toxins and helps to keep you mind sharp. The brain and heart alone are composed of 73% water. It's no wonder why water is essential to your livelihood.

8. **Get plenty of rest:** You've heard it said many times before, "Get more rest". However, this is often

easier said than done. But you can change this by prioritizing sleep as part of your daily routine. One way to do this is by cutting out things you do in the evening that might keep you awake at night, such as watching late night television or scrolling through your electronic devices (i.e., your phone or tablet).

Set a bedtime and stick to it. If you have young kids in the house, keep them on a routine so that you can maintain your sleeping routine. Most importantly, don't exhaust yourself. Listen to your body if you feel like you're overly tired and give yourself permission to rest.

9. **Control Your Environment: Eliminate Negative Influences in Your Life**

There's so much chaos happening in the world that it's easy for us to feel as though we have no control over our lives. But the reality is, you have control over the principal part of your world - your surrounding environment.

By controlling your surrounding environment, you greatly reduce your chances of failure. This is because you alone dictate what and who you will surround yourself with. When you do this, you control the type of energy around you and choose where to put your focus.

You can achieve a clear mind by getting rid the things that distract you or bring negativity into your life. For example, if your co-workers do nothing but gossip in the breakroom at work, don't join in. Choose to have lunch in a space where you can keep a clear head and recharge.

If you have friends who do nothing but complain to you about their woes without ever uplifting you in any areas of your life, consider re-evaluating what you want out of your friendships.

A negative environment is just as toxic as poisonous food. It impacts your thinking and your well-being. In other words, your external state impacts your internal state. The fastest way to kill your light is to surround yourself with negative people and influences. Be mindful of the things you watch, what you listen to, what you read, and who you surround yourself with.

Always surround yourself with positive influences that bring out the best in you.

10. Strengthen your faith and meditate:
You must constantly remind yourself of what you believe in so that your faith remains strong. What is it that you believe God has in store for you and how

are you reinforcing this promise in your life? Do you have a prayer life? Are you reading scripture? Are you meditating? If you feel that your faith is running low, it is important to restore your faith. Your faith is what gives you hope in what it is you believe in and working towards.

When your faith weakens, so does your belief in yourself and everything you've envisioned. Realign with God and everything will start clicking.

Meditation is a great way to focus your attention on your faith and the things that matter most. The process of meditation is peaceful, enriching, and calming, and also helps to reduce stress. Most importantly, meditation helps you to gain a better perspective on the things that are happening in your life so that you can seek the necessary guidance.

When you feel unmotivated or uninspired, plug into the right source. Meditate and check in within yourself the same way you check in with your best friend or closest family members. Meditation cleanses mind, which is where your thoughts are stored.

Make it a practice to meditate just as you would clean your home.

SETTING BOUNDARIES THAT WORK

Setting boundaries allows you to practice self-care without making any compromises. We've all been experienced having set aside 'me-time' or plans to relax, only to forfeit is because we've made an exception for something or something that was not a priority in that moment. Maybe you set aside time to meditate but something came up that made you lose your focus. Or maybe you made plans to eat healthy for the day, but someone bought a box of donuts to the office and told you that you just had to try them.

Maybe someone said or did something to you that was completely disrespectful, but you didn't address it because you didn't want to cause any conflict or offend the other person. Though this might not seem like a big deal, if you're not careful, the lack of boundaries actually opens the door to mental and emotional abuse. Without boundaries, it's easy for you to self-sabotage and lose sight of taking care of yourself.

Much like controlling your environment, setting boundaries allows you to regain power over your life. It is a process that allows you to set your own rules and regulations that for what you will and won't accept. You call your own shots and set your own limits. Setting boundaries is not only liberating, but empowering, which does wonders for boosting your self-esteem.

It signals self-confidence in that you know what you want, and you have no intentions to settle for less.

Establishing healthy boundaries also influences the way people relate with you because you set the precedent for how you want to be treated. When you have clear boundaries for yourself, people around you also become clear on your expectations. This is why it's important that you don't make exceptions for the boundaries that you set for yourself. Identify them, make them plain, and adhere to them at all cost.

Think about the boundaries that you set for yourself as a form of accountability. The more steadfast you are in adhering to your boundaries, the better you'll care for yourself in the long run.

When you adhere to your boundaries, you signify that you love and value yourself so much that you care enough to establish clear standards to protect your environment, your mind, and your well-being. Here are some key areas where you should take time to establish clear boundaries in your life:

1. House rules—what you expect from your spouse and/or children, and guests in your home environment.
2. Communication—the level of communication you expect from family members, significant others, clients and/or co-workers.

3. Respect—the manner which you expect (and allow) others to treat you.
4. Personal space—what you consider to be a respectable distance regarding your physical space vs. what is too close for comfort.
5. Use of your time—what you consider to be a reasonable use of your time by your own standards and those around you.

TOP TEN BENEFITS OF BOUNDARIES AND SELF-LOVE

1. It increases your level of self-acceptance.
2. It boosts your self-esteem and self-confidence.
3. It helps you to make wiser choices.
4. It helps you to practice self-discipline.
5. It helps you to practice accountability.
6. It helps you to remain focused on your vision.
7. It helps you to maintain a positive mindset.
8. It strengthens your relationships with others.
9. It prevents tolerance for emotional and mental abuse.
10. It helps to maintains a healthy mind, body, and spirit.

RELATIONSHIPS AND BOUNDARIES

All too often, women overlook the impacts of their relationships on their well-being. Your personal and professional relationships influence your self-esteem, your priorities, how you spend your time, and the decisions you make. This is why it's important to distinguish between the types of relationships you have and develop boundaries for each of them.

You need to be clear on the role that each of your relationships play in your life, what influences they have over you, and whether they support or hinder you. Your relationships matter. The people you surround yourself with and the relationships can impact your future for the better or for worse, which is why strong boundaries are so important.

Here is a comprehensive list of "do's" and "don'ts" when determining the types of relationships you should keep in your efforts to sustain self-care.

Do's and Don'ts in Determining the Relationships in Your Life

- Don't surround yourself with people who project their fears onto you.
- Surround yourself with people who see the best in you—they highlight your potential, not constantly point out your flaws.

- Surround yourself with optimistic people who have the ability to see the silver lining in even the worst of situations.

- Surround yourself with people who are willing to share their knowledge with you and want to see you grow.

- Surround yourself with forward-thinking people who encourage you to focus more on your future than your past.

- Don't surround yourself with people who are overly cynical about everything and have little faith in nothing.

- Surround yourself with people who affirm you in a positive light—through their words and actions.

- Don't surround yourself by people who make you feel insecure or "lesser than" through their words or actions (i.e., making negative comments about your appearance, proclaiming that you don't know what you're doing, dismissing your dreams, verbally disrespecting you, physically violating you).

- Surround yourself with people who will tell you the truth in love—people who provide constructive criticism in a way that is respectful and elevates you to become better.

- Don't surround yourself with people who make you feel you can't be yourself.

- Surround yourself with people who make you feel good about yourself.
- Surround yourself with people who make you laugh.
- Surround yourself with people who encourage you to have fun and try new things.
- Don't surround yourself with people who don't celebrate your fault; instead, they fault your for making positive changes in your life.
- Don't surround yourself with people who are threatened by your growth—they want you to stay the same and feel as though you're leaving them behind.
- Surround yourself with people who genuinely love and care for you.

MAINTANING HEALTHY RELATIONSHIPS

Believe it or not, maintaining healthy relationships are an important part of our well-being. Relationships play a huge role in our professional and personal lives.

As humans we are social creatures, and therefore need positive interactions with others as a necessity, just as we do food and water. Research has shown that meaningful social that people who have satisfying relationships with family, friends, and their community are happier, have fewer health problems, and live longer.

Conversely, a relative lack of social ties or meaningful relationships is associated with depression and later-life cognitive decline. The lack of meaningful social connection is also associated with increased mortality. One study, which examined data from more than 309,000 people, found that lack of strong relationships increased the risk of premature death from all causes by 50%.

There are several reasons behind this. One of the most powerful is that meaningful social interactions help to relieve harmful levels of stress, which can adversely affect coronary arteries, gut function, insulin regulation, and the immune system. Caring behaviors from others also trigger the release of stress-reducing hormones. The same is true when we care for others in return.

Though relationships are beneficial to your health, they can take a lot of time and energy. The better you understand how to develop and maintain your relationships, the easier it is to facilitate them. Whether you're working to build a more meaningful relationship with your spouse or significant other, your boss, co-workers and team members, family members, community members, or closest friends, here are key building blocks to help ensure your relationships are positive and meaningful:

- **Trust** – the ability to depend on others with confidence in their feelings, words, and actions. Trust creates safety and builds confidence.
- **Respect** – mutual regard for one another's thoughts, feelings, wishes, and abilities. Respect reinforces trust.

- **Mindfulness** – the ability to be cognizant and considerate of each other's thoughts and feelings in everything you say and do. At work: How will this decision impact the rest of the team? At home: How will my mate feel if I don't visit the in-laws this weekend?

- **Open communication** – the ability to communicate freely about any and everything at any time. There are no restrictions with regard to what can be shared between you, nor should there be any reservation about openly sharing.

Open communication includes the ability to be open to each other's perspective. This is why diversity and inclusion are so instrumental to a good work environment. It allows a variety of views and perspectives that produce more possible solutions which ultimately help achieve the best possible outcomes. The same is true for exploring each other's perspectives in a personal relationship, such as making decisions at home. A good example of this might be deciding how to best spend quality time or deciding on parenting styles.

- **Active Listening:** Effective communication requires strong listening skills. Communication is just as much about hearing what the other person has to say as it is about being heard. Active listening requires you to demonstrate that you actually hear and understand what each other has to say without distraction. In other words, you can recite it back, clarify what it being said, and act on what is being said accordingly.

- **Emotional Intelligence** – If you want to develop meaningful relationships at home or at work, you must master how to tap into your own emotions. Being aware your own emotions is vital to your relationships because it allow you to better receive and understand the needs of others. It improves your ability to communicate and increases your ability to seek to understand.

- **Time and appreciation** – It's important for you to make time for your relationships so that they can flourish and grow. For example, unless you spend time with your co-workers, you only appreciate them for the job that they do, not for who they are.

When you take the time to get to know who they really are, your working relationship becomes much more meaningful and impactful.

The same is true for your romantic relationships. It's important to take the time to continuously get to know one another. The time that you spend with someone also symbolizes how much appreciate them.

Appreciation is also key to maintaining healthy relationships with others. Appreciation, whether verbal or tangible, demonstrates that you value the other person. Relationships are strongest when both parties feel valued.

Healthy relationships have many benefits.

In addition to providing us with companionship and helping us to live longer, they allow us to step out of our own shell and appreciate others around us. If you maintain the right boundaries, your relationships can lead you to be more self-seeking, understanding, and creative.

ADDRESSING STRESS AND ANXIETY

Managing stress and anxiety is a critical part of maintaining a healthy mind and body. It is a major component of self-care that many women overlook or simply take for granted. Stress makes us feel overwhelmed and stuck. The truth is, when you're stuck, you're really afraid, and stress is the achiever word for fear. According to the National Institute of Mental Health, almost one out of five adults will suffer from an anxiety disorder in a given year.

Furthermore, the psychiatric literature reports over 100 phobias, disorders which manifest in a persistent and irrational fear of objects or situations. This type of anxiety is especially prevalent among women. If unaddressed, it can hinder you from living your fullest potential. Your light will never shine as bright as it should if you don't learn to get your levels of stress and anxiety under control.

It's important to start by gaining a full understanding of what stress really is.

Stress can be defined as any type of change that causes physical, emotional, or psychological strain in response to a challenge or demand; it's how your brain and body responds to situations like these. Examples might include a public performance or speaking engagement, having to deliver a presentation at work, trying to meet the demand of raising children, trying to secure a home loan, or working through a rough patch in your marriage. Stress can also be caused by significant life changes or traumatic events.

Whatever your stressors are, they can negatively impact your health, which is why it is important to pay attention to how you deal with minor and major stressors and determine when to seek help.

Everyone experiences stress to some degree. The way you respond to stress, however, makes a big difference to your overall well-being. It's perfectly normal to experience low levels of stress. However, too much stress can lead to burnout, hormonal changes, mental distress, and strain on your physical organs.

Stress can also contribute to anxiety, which is characterized as frequently having intense, excessive, and persistent worry and fear about everyday situations. It consists of irrational fear, and avoidance of situations that provide little to no threat of danger and is our response to an unknown source or perhaps the experience of stress. Again, everyone experiences some level of anxiety.

However, constant and unsubstantiated worry about everyday circumstances can interferes with daily life and might even be a sign of an anxiety disorder.

Here are some common examples of high stress levels and anxiety:
1. Sweating
2. Poor memory
3. Restlessness
4. Impatience
5. Hyperventilation
6. Feeling that you have to readily escape
7. Being fearful
8. Feeling on edge

When your body senses that there is a threat, it will respond automatically with shallow breaths, racing thoughts, and tensed muscles. These are wonderful things when you are in danger but can be very disruptive if experiences in situations that are conventionally safe.

If you want to successfully monitor your levels of stress and anxiety, you must first seek to understand your feelings and experiences. Your feelings might be complex, but they are valid, and it is important to understand why they are what they are. Much of this goes back to understanding your emotional triggers. When you are feeling anxious, pay special attention to the following types of triggers:

- Internal stimuli responses
- Emotions (worry)
- Mental Images (replaying interactions)

- Physical state (racing heartbeat)
- Thoughts (I might not get the promotion)
- External stimuli
- Presence of others (social events)
- Physical setting (a classroom)
- Social Pressure
- Activities (going to a dinner party)

Are you feeling anxious because you've been hurt? Are you scared or have feelings of being trapped because of a past traumatic experience? Doing this type of work is a great first step to combating your anxiety. If working through a traumatic event becomes overwhelming for you, try doing so in small steps.

Here are a few questions you can ask yourself to help you work through it:

1. What was the distressing event?
2. Where was it?
3. Who was there?
4. What did your body feel?
5. How did your emotions change?
6. What were your instincts?
7. What went through your mind?

Being aware of your triggers can both help you reduce high stress situations and manage your anxiety when you find yourself in situations that are beyond your control. When you find yourself in a high stress situation and you feel anxiety coming on, try doing the following:

1. **Breathing Exercises:** Position yourself in a comfortable state and place a hand on your stomach and chest. Inhale and feel your belly rise with oxygen, and completely focus your attention to your stomach when it falls. Eliminate the distractions around you and focus on your inner feeling and thoughts until you feel centered again. This promotes mindfulness and allows you to refocus.

2. **Affirmations and Manifestations:** Positive affirmations are a powerful way to care for your subconscious and our wellbeing. Speak life into yourself when you're feeling dark, stressed or afraid. Tell yourself, "You're strong; you don't need to be afraid", "Everything's going to be ok", "You're going to get through this". It is a tool to teach ourselves how to be successful in both personal and professional ways.

   Repeat these things to yourself as many times as necessary until you feel calm and centered again.

3. **Alternative feelings, thoughts, and behaviors:** Consider whether your stress and anxieties might be about other feelings. Could there be another situation that is causing you to project your past feelings onto the current one? Could there be any more positives in this situation that you are ignoring? You can develop alternate responses to your thoughts and feelings by practicing grounding exercises.

You should also take time to assess whether you're looking at the whole picture. Sometimes we focus on small parts of a situation that cause us stress, rather than consider helpful ways to view the bigger picture. Alternative behaviors allow you to focus on things that you can do in your moments of stress that would be more beneficial to your mind than obsessing over the matter.

Replace anxiety-filled thoughts, predictions, and exaggerations that result in unhealthy behaviors with positive thoughts that produce healthy, productive behaviors. Always remember that worry consists of the negative thoughts in your mind; anxiety is when you allow those thoughts to control how you feel.

COGNITIVE DISTORTIONS AND STRESS

When tend to exaggerate stressful circumstances and tell ourselves things like, "I'm such a failure" or "This will never change for the better". This style of thinking is often completely unwarranted and only contributes to unnecessary stress. It's a phenomenon referred to as cognitive distortion.

When you find yourself doing this, make it a practice to replace these distortions with positive affirmations. Here is a list of behaviors that are characteristic of cognitive distortions and are commonly seen among women:

- All or nothing thinking – "If I am not perfect, I have failed".

- Over-generalizing – "nothing good ever happens".

- Mental filter – Noticing your failures but not seeing your successes.

- Disqualifying the positive – "This success does not count to me".

- Jumping to conclusions – Assuming what others think, and what will happen in the future.

- Magnification and minimization - Blowing things out of, or shrinking them out of, proportion.

- Emotional Reasoning – "I feel so embarrassed, so I must be an idiot".

- The "Should and Must" – "I should have been able to be there for her".
- Labeling – "I am such a loser".
- Personalization – "This is all my fault".

You can apply the success cycle—Potential-action-results—to help you with this. You have to see the potential in things so that you don't distort them or get discouraged. There's a saying that goes, "Get in your head and you're dead". You'll never find your purpose in your head. Get in tune with your heart, and your mind will follow suit.

Shine Your Light: Self-Reflection

Take time to answer the following questions.

1. Are you practicing self-care the way that you should? Why or why not? What can you do more of?
2. Are you taking care of your body by exercising, eating, and sleeping well?
3. How do you protect your peace?
4. How good are you at controlling your environment?
5. What boundaries do you have in place to help you practice self-love and self-care?
6. Do your relationships promote or hinder your self-care?

LET YOUR LIGHT SHINE
Becoming the **Best Version** of Yourself

Chapter - 06

TRIUMPH DESPITE LOST DREAMS

"Our set-backs are often our set-ups for what's to come".

There is no bigger threat to living your best life than feeling like you've lost your dream. It happens to all of us at one point or another for various reasons. The most common include major life changes that make it easy to get lost in the fast pace of life. This might be attributed to changing careers, getting married and having children, or perhaps even having to take care of an aging parent.

Another common contributor is experiencing failure or great disappointment. Sometimes, when we feel defeated enough, we give up on our dream and convince ourselves that it's not worth revisiting because it will cause too much heartache and pain. When you finally decide to try again, you feel like it's been lost and impossible to get it back.

However, God wants to repurpose your mess and make it a masterpiece. Your dreams are never really lost. At best, they are buried deep down inside of you, hidden in the dark and covered in dust. You didn't lose motivation, you lost focus on what's most important. It's up to you to refocus, turn your light on, and dust your dream off so that you can bring it back to life.

DEALING WITH GRIEF AND LOSS
Many times, women give up on their dreams because they experience loss so great that they lose sight of their purpose and vision. In this case, it's important to recognize your

grief it's important to recognize your grief and work towards healing so that you can live your dream again.

Grief is a natural response to loss. It's the emotional suffering you feel when something or someone you love is taken away. You may associate grief with the death of a loved one, the loss of a job, or even a divorce. The more significant the loss, the more intense the grief. However, even subtle losses can lead to grief, such as moving away from home or retiring from a career you loved. Everyone grieves differently.

How you grieve depends on many factors, including your personality and coping style, your life experience, your faith, the nature of the loss, and your support system. The grieving process takes time. It's important to remember that the grieving process takes time; it won't happen overnight. For some, it takes weeks. For others, it takes months on years. Whatever your grief experience, it's important to be patient with yourself and allow the process to naturally unfold.

If you're trying hard to restore the passion you once had for your dream but you're experiencing any of the following, it may be because you're still working through your stages of grief. There are five stages of grief are as follows:
1. Denial: "This can't be happening to me."
2. Anger: "Why is this happening? Who is to blame?"

3. Bargaining: "Make this not happen, and in return I will _____."
4. Depression: "I'm too sad to do anything."
5. Acceptance: "I'm at peace with what happened."

Keep in mind that these stages are completely natural. However, restoring your dream can be difficult without understanding how to manage these stages appropriately. Understanding the symptoms associated with grief and the various stages can help put you on a path to healing and restoring your dream.

Common symptoms of grief include:

- Shock and disbelief – feeling like you're crazy, numb, or in a bad dream.
- Sadness – feelings of emptiness, despair, yearning, deep loneliness or persistent crying.
- Guilt – You may regret or feel guilty about things you did or didn't say or do, even if there's nothing you could have done to prevent the loss.
- Anger – feel angry and resentful at yourself or someone else, even if no one is at fault.
- Fear – feeling anxious, helpless, or insecure. alone.
- Physical symptoms – fatigue, nausea, lowered immunity, weight loss or weight gain, aches and pains, and insomnia.

If you are experiencing any of these symptoms during your time of grief, it's important that you take the right steps to manage them to ensure your well-being. Key actions you should take include:

- **Get support**. Find people you can talk to and rely on, such as friends, family members, members of your community, and faith-based organizations. It's not always easy to open up to others but sharing yourself can help to carry the burden. Joining a support group or talking to a professional therapist can also serve a significant source of support.

- **Draw from your faith**. Pray, meditate, strengthen your belief, and find hope and purpose.

- **Express your feelings:** Don't shy away from your feelings of sadness, anger, or guilt. Acknowledge your feelings and find creative ways to express them. You might do this through journaling, painting, music, or even poetry. The more you express your feelings, the easier it will become to face them and move through them.

LOST DREAMS CAN ALWAYS BE FOUND

Whether you've experienced a traumatic loss or you've been defeated by disappointment and failure, your dream is not lost. You may not be able to regain lost time, but you can control what happens with the time you have remaining. Everything you've been through, with all of its ups and downs is for a purpose. Did you ever stop to think that maybe your life experiences, good and bad, were designed to propel your dream forward? Many times, we go through hardships that were designed to make us stronger and wiser so that our dream becomes a success.

Dust your dream off and begin taking the necessary steps to actualize it. Don't sit and wallow in sorrow because you cannot imagine how you got to where you are right now. You did what you thought was best at every point in your life, and there is nothing to be sorry about. Put your regrets aside and embrace what you have now. If you have breath in your body and a functioning mind, you are capable of pushing your dream forward.

If you look deeply into yourself, your dreams were never really lost; they were just suppressed. That picture of the best you that you can be, which your mind conceived many years ago, is still in the corner of your mind. The challenge is bringing it to the forefront. You can do this by taking the time to reflect on what you want and acknowledging that you are deserving and capable of achieving it.

Your dream is beautiful, it's wonderful, and serves a great purpose. Denying the purpose that is within you is greater than any tragedy of the past or fear of tragedy that might arise in the future. Denying yourself of your dream is the ultimate tragedy.

Stop convincing yourself that it's too late, you're too old, or that no one will take you seriously.

Allow yourself to be immersed in the process of finding your dreams. Give yourself room for your lost dream to come back to you. Reflect, reflect, and reflect some more! Revel in the feeling your dream gives you—excitement, joy, and a sense of purpose. Hold on to that feeling and write it down.

Try answering the following questions:
1. What is it that you once wanted to do that you let get away from you?
2. Why did you put your dream on the back burner?
3. What excuses have you been telling yourself about why your dream is no longer possible?
4. If your dream were a reality, how would it make you feel? How would it change your live and the lives of those around you?

Don't be overwhelmed by the size or magnitude of your dream. No matter how big your dream might seem, let it take hold of you, and hold onto it in return.

It's possible to become so guarded that you condition your mind to shut your dream out. Even if your dream scares you, allow yourself to feel that fear and welcome the opportunity to take on the challenge. Rather than running from your dream because of fear, allow the fear of missing out on your dream to motivate you.

IT'S NEVER TOO LATE TO TRIUMPH OVER YOUR DREAMS

Women have a terrible habit of setting unnecessary, and sometimes, unrealistic timelines by when things they should achieve certain things in their lives. For example, it's not uncommon for women to feel they need to be married and have children by a certain age. They feel less than accomplished if they haven't achieved a promotion after a certain number of years, are if they haven't established a business of their own by a certain stage in their lives. These are all false expectations.

The truth is, there is a time and place for everything in our lives. Furthermore, your timing isn't necessarily the same as everyone else's timing. You're running your race. This means it's impossible for you not to be a winner, no matter what time you arrive at the finish line.

The only failure is not running the race at all.

Maybe you've already started the race, but you feel like it's too late to make changes. This is another huge misconception that can cause you to lose sight of your dream. The only thing certain in life is change. Change prevents us from being stagnant. This is true for our relationships, the way we run our businesses, how we approach our jobs, and even the way we parent.

Change is a constant in our lives and should be welcomed, not feared. Change your priorities, change your mindset, change your routine, and change the way you approach challenges. This is a sign of maturity and growth, which is an ongoing process throughout every stage of our lives. It's never too late for change. In fact, it may be the very thing you need to bring your dream back to life.

DEALING WITH SETBACKS

Success is never found without setbacks. You will most certainly encounter challenges and obstacles when working towards your dream. The key is to understand how to address them and make them work for your benefit. For example, when you apply your makeup and don't get your foundation quite right, you don't throw it all away, you simply wash it off and take the necessary steps to reapply it. If you make a cup of coffee and it isn't quite sweet enough, you don't toss it out, you add more sugar.

If you're working on a major presentation for work and you're not happy with some of your content, you don't decide to not give the presentation at all, you alter the presentation so that it is suitable for your company's needs.

The key is to view your setbacks as opportunities, rather than view them as the enemy. A setback doesn't mean it's the end of the road, it's simply an opportunity to pause and regroup...and possibly move forward in a way that will result in an even better outcome than you originally anticipated.

Here are some tips to help you plan for and deal with setbacks:

1. **Set achievable goals:** Even if your dream is larger than life, make it a practice to take small steps towards achieving them. Categorize your short-term and long-term goals and prioritize them accordingly. Your long-term goals can be said to be the big picture, while your short-term goals are the little things you can do to get you closer to the bigger picture.

   You can prevent feeling overwhelmed and unnecessary feelings of defeat by ensuring that your goals are realistic and by pacing yourself along the way.

2. **Learn from past experiences:** embrace failures, mistakes, and even disappointments as opportunities to learn and grow. Consider ways that you can do things differently so that you don't fall into the same traps as you did in the past.

   Consider what did and didn't work in your previous relationships, your parenting style, or how you implemented your business plan and identify ways that you can build upon what you now know that you otherwise would not have known without your previous experiences. Your previous experiences are part of who you are. Learn to embrace them and use them in a way that lifts you up, rather than allowing them to weigh you down.

3. **Be patient:** Patience is a virtue and one that you desperately need in the actualizing of dreams. Not everything will go exactly as planned, and that's ok. Remember that good things in life come to those who wait. Some things take time and some longer than others. Don't allow impatience to cause you to be discouraged. Slow and steady is the race. Success cannot be rushed; it takes time and diligence.

4. **Motivate yourself and remain focused:** We commonly respond to setbacks by being discouraged or easily distracted. In fact, we can

become so distracted that we readily begin looking for something else to do when things don't go our way, especially if it's something that seems to be working for someone else. Remember, your journey to achieving your dream is as unique as your dream itself. Don't expect for journey to be like anyone else's. More importantly, don't wait for anyone else to motivate you. You've got to cheer for yourself first because most people won't cheer for you until you've made it.

Remain focused on your dream and motivate yourself along the way. Don' be discouraged. It isn't hard for you now because you're doing it wrong, it's extra hard for you now because you're finally doing it right! Remember to practice positive affirmations and celebrate your accomplishments as you go as a way to recharge and boost your esteem. Remain positive and rest assured that your efforts are not in vein, despite the setbacks you might encounter.

5. **Be persistent:** Set your mind on your dream and why it matters to you, and commit to it, no matter what. Keep pushing, no matter the circumstances. Quitting is never an option. Consider your dream your lifeline; keep it charged and running. You have to start keeping the promises you make to yourself.

You can find your dream and triumph over it if you commit to nurturing it. You are a warrior. There is nothing you can't achieve. Shine your light, rise above your loss, and find meaning again.

Shine Your Light: Self-Reflection

Take time to answer the following questions.

1. What dream have you put aside and why?
2. Have you experienced loss or disappointment that has left you feeling discouraged or defeated?
3. Are you experiencing any stages of grief? If so, have you sought out the necessary support?
4. When you reflect on your dream, what about it gives you hope and joy?
5. What excuses do you tell yourself about why you can't bring your dream back to life?
6. How can you motivate yourself to revive your dream and triumph?

LET YOUR LIGHT SHINE
Becoming the **Best Version** of Yourself

Chapter - 07

UNMASKING THE GREATNESS WITHIN

"Greatness & convenient don't coexist".

You were created to do great things. There is a seed of greatness that has been implanted in you. It is up to you to water and germinate it so that it is manifested in your life. in our lives. The key to becoming successful is to live out your purpose. When understand your purpose, your vision becomes clear, and your dream becomes attainable. If you're having trouble identifying what that is, you have some soul-searching to do.

Finding your purpose is the business of figuring out what you were put on this earth to do. Your purpose is tied to your very existence. Without it, your life is meaningless. And without meaning, you cannot manifest the greatness within you. Living your life without purpose is like having energy with nowhere to focus it. Your greatness should not be underestimated because your happiness and ability to make a difference in the world depends on it.

Your purpose is what unmasks your greatness and makes life worth living for.

UNMASKING YOUR PURPOSE

Purpose is more about your life's journey than it is the destination. What difference will you make? How many lives will you touch along the way?

So, how do you find it? The key to find what drives you. What is the thing that you enjoy that also fills your life with meaning?

Consider the following questions:

1. What do you look forward to every day?
2. What is it that you enjoy that you can never see yourself getting tired of?
3. What is it that you can get lost in without having track of time?
4. What is it that you're capable of doing or producing that seems more like fun than work?
5. What is it about what could be that constantly consumes your thoughts?
6. What changes do you want to see in the world?
7. What difference do you want to make in the lives of others?

These are all questions you can ask yourself to help you identify your purpose—what you're passionate about, what gets you out of bed in the morning, what you live for. Don't look for what you can do to have purpose, look at what you're already doing that is purposeful.

Don't use not fully understanding your purpose as an excuse not to start walking in your greatness. GPS doesn't work if you only have a destination. You have to start with where you are. Also, don't limit yourself to one thing. Who says you can't have multiple destinations as part of your life's journey? Your dreams should be plentiful. Write down 5 dreams every single morning to continue the work of unmasking your purpose. If you use the greatness inside of you to give your all to what is next, things will open up.

CHANGE YOUR MINDSET

Even once you've discovered your purpose, you can't exercise your greatness without changing your mindset. This is because your thoughts control your actions, and your actions determine your success. Your mindset is shaped by several internal and external influences, such as what you observed, what you hear, the messages you give yourself based on your self-esteem, what you feel, and what you perceive.

You can change your mindset by commanding your thoughts. This requires understanding them, controlling what you allow to influence them, and reinforcing positive messages.

Understanding your thoughts: Much like understanding your emotional triggers, it's important that you take the time to understand why you think the way you do. You may have a certain perception of yourself and the world around you based on what you were taught as a child.

Perhaps your thoughts have been shaped by past experiences or the way you've interpreted things based on how you felt or how you perceived things that you might not necessarily have understood. Examine where your thoughts stem from and whether they have a negative or positive effect on your life.

Keep in mind the concept of manifestation when you do this. When you think negatively, you give unconsciously give yourself permission to display negative habits and behaviors. When you think positively, you welcome positive energy and pursue positive actions. Take the time to understand your thoughts and their impact on your life so that you can adjust your thinking where necessary.

It's so important to keep track of your positive thoughts, especially innovative ones. Take the time each day to connect with your thoughts. Realize when you have those best thoughts and carve out time to focus & collect them.

Monitor your influences: the people and things around you can influence the way you think. For example, if you were told as a child that all men are the same, you might approach every relationship as though there's no good man out there to be found. Likewise, if you were told that women rarely become rarely achieve positions of leadership in your field of work, chances are, you'll believe you're not capable of achieving a promotion that you may very well deserve.

You can monitor this by controlling the messages that you allowed to influence you and challenging them. You can do this by controlling what you read, the music you listen to, and even the messages that you receive while watching certain content on TV. Even social media can influence positive or negative thinking. If the only content you follow on social media promotes tearing other people down, your mind automatically takes a negative shift in how it formulates your thoughts about others in reality.

On the contrary, if the content you follow on social media promotes philanthropy or spreading love, you're more apt to apply these concepts in your everyday life. Your self-image is also influenced by the images you subject yourself to, including print and media. The more positive images you receive and associate with yourself, the more highly you think of yourself.

In addition to the content you receive, consider whether the people who surround you feed you negative or positive messages, whether directly or indirectly. For example, if someone close to you dismisses your ideas as silly or achievable, it might contribute to negative thoughts about your capabilities.

Likewise, if you dress you best for a date and never receive a compliment, it might lead you to think negatively about your appearance.

Reinforce positive thinking: it's important that you nurture your mindset just as you would your body to keep it healthy. This requires you to reinforce positive messages and positive thinking. You can do this by listening to motivational podcasts, subscribing to motivational newsletters, joining book clubs, networking with people who share the same goals as you, working with a mentor, and only surrounding yourself with people who uplift you.

If you really want to reinforce your positive thinking, write it down and put it into motion. You can do this by recording positive or happy thoughts, reciting motivational quotes, and highlighting and revisiting messages that motivate you while reading a book.

Exercise your willpower: It is inevitable that negative thoughts will try to pay a visit. It happens to all of us. One negative thought creeps in and then others follow suit. The best way to deter this is to acknowledge the thought and take the time to understand why it surfaced in the first place.

When you dismiss it, you unconsciously give yourself permission to welcome these thoughts in the future. Remember, this is how self-sabotage often comes into play. Once you have a handle on your negative thoughts, the next step is to put them in their place. Do not allow these thoughts to determine how you feel about yourself and certainly not how you behave.

Exercise your willpower in not giving into negative thoughts by allowing these them to take control over your feelings or your actions. Make it a practice to replace them with positive thoughts and affirmations. Exercising your willpower allows you to care for your subconscious so that you can achieve the greatness that is within you. Make this your mantra, "I'm okay. I'm safe. And I'm loved".

FINDING THE GREATNESS WITHIN

1. **Be honest with yourself**: All change starts with honesty. If you really want to uncover your greatness, you have to start by being honest with yourself. Honesty allows you to drop a pin on where you are and starts the momentum to where you are going. However, this is one of the hardest things for women to do. Why? Because we are often taught that we have a place or role in society—in a marriage, at work, in motherhood, and so on.

   As a result, we find ourselves living in the shadows of expectations that we didn't set for ourselves and hiding the true parts of ourselves.

   However, it's important to set external expectations of you aside and be brutally honest about what's inside of you and what you want out of life. This includes your experiences, your wants and desires, how you feel about yourself, and even acknowledging areas that feel broken or incomplete.

If you find this hard to do, you are not alone. Being in touch with the most private areas of ourselves can sometimes make us feel like we're on an island and can even be uncomfortable. However, without this type of honesty, the falsehoods that you've embedded in your subconscious will inevitably be projected into your life and onto others.

Commit to doing the work. What thoughts do you have that no one else knows about? What experiences have you had that you don't speak on? What private fears do you have that you feel no one else will understand? This is the work that is required of you before you can walk in the purpose that was designed for your life.

2. **Explore and try new things:** Try new things to discover interests you might not know you have. You'd be surprised at how much you enjoy things you never knew you did simply because you never tried. The same is true for discovering your talents. The best way to get to know what you're great at is to explore.

   Don't just explore your current passions. Make it a point to try as many new things as possible as regularly as you can. This will help broaden your horizon of knowledge and incorporate better approaches to the passion you might have decided to pursue. It will also help you to retain the excitement and enthusiasm of pursuing your goals.

When we limit ourselves to the same way of doing things, we become bored and risk losing the passion we once had. We all love a good challenge because it keeps us on our toes and gives us a sense of excitement. After all, finding the greatness within you should be nothing short of exciting. Get out of your comfort zone and push your own limits.

The more you challenge yourself, the more you grow. Exploring new ways of doing things can both help you to adopt new skills and improve skills you already have.

3. **Decide what kind of legacy you want to leave behind:** There's no better way to find the greatness within than to think about the legacy you want to leave behind. Everyone wants their life to count for something. How will your life count? How is it that you want to be remembered? What is it that would bring you great joy to know you've achieved it before you left this earth?

What is it that you want to pass down to your children? What difference do you want to make in your community? Your legacy isn't necessarily anything tangible. It is the difference that you make in this world and how your actions today will live on for future generations to come.

4. **Listen to your heart and pursue your dream:** The heart is the sanctuary of all your passions and desires. There is no better guide in life than you heart. Unlike external influences, your will guide to where you truly want to be because it is always true itself. You just need to be true to it. This is why it's important to guard your heart so that it isn't filled with the wrong things or abused by people who don't mean it well.

If you keep your heart pure and listen to it carefully, it will tell you exactly where your passion lies. Just as faith without works is dead, so is purpose without passion. Your heart might sometimes lead you in a direction that feels unfamiliar. But don't let this scare you because your faith coupled with the desires of your heart will never steer you wrong.

Once you're clear on the direction you need to move in, start moving! Learn and do all you can to pursue your dream. Your dream won't just come to you because it's in your heart; you have to work for it.

5. **Don't stop learning:** Success doesn't come easy; it takes hard work. You must be willing to put in the necessary work in your pursuit of happiness. This means continually working on yourself and your craft. You should never stop learning about who you are as a person and how to improve.

Read books, listen to podcasts, enroll in classes, participate in trainings, watch tutorials, and network with other women. This is all part of your personal development, which is necessary in pursuing the greatness that is inside of you.

As a woman of purpose, you must work on every aspect of your life, such as your knowledge of what you're pursuing, your character, and your ability to take risks. Just as the world evolves, so must you. When you become static, you welcome the idea of settling for less.

When you operate based on the greatness that is inside of you, you don't settle, you break barriers. The more you learn, the more you realize the greatness that's inside of you, and the more skilled you become at implementing your vision. We are learners, not failures. Discouragement just means you gave up on learning.

6. **Allow yourself to blossom:** Give yourself permission to be wildly successful. Give yourself permission to grow, despite the growth or opinions of everyone else around you. Even flowers change depending on the season. The greatest change of all is when they begin to blossom. Water the seeds of love and greatness that are within you. Don't worry about whether you're ready or qualified. God doesn't call the qualified, he qualifies the called. When you're "not ready" is usually when you're ready. If you have a dream within you, you're ready to start moving on it.

Shine Your Light: Self-Reflection
Take time to answer the following questions.

1. Do you take the time to collect your thoughts and reflect on them each day?
2. Have you taken time to explore your purpose? What is it that brings meaning to your life?
3. Are you honest with yourself about who you are and what you want out of life? If not, what's holding you back from living your truth?
4. What legacy do you want to leave behind, long after you're gone?
5. Do you make it a point to learn something new every day?

Have you given yourself permission to be wildly successful? Do you put limitation on your success? If so, why?

LET YOUR LIGHT SHINE

Becoming the **Best Version** of Yourself

Chapter - 08

THE ROLE OF SELF-CONFIDENCE IN PERSONAL AND PROFESSIONAL FULFILLMENT

"How you live today builds the confidence you need for tomorrow".

The subject of confidence is a very delicate one for women. We're either dragged for not having enough confidence or frowned upon for having too much of it. When women are highly confident, they are termed "aggressive" instead of being referred to as bold. In exhibiting confidence and speaking up for themselves, women are often deemed "bossy" or "rebellious", rather than leaders.

This is where the divide comes in regarding how we reverence confidence in men compared to women. Women have historically been viewed as nurturers who primary responsibility is to care for their husbands and children. Images of strength and power are not associated with women.

The narrative that most women are given, even as little girls, is that they are the supporter, not the leader; their voice doesn't really matter; and they're not strong enough to take on the challenges of the world without the help of a man. Everyone need help from someone at some point in life, whether it be a spouse, a family member, or a friend.

However, the belief that you must be fully dependent on someone else in order to survive is very unhealthy. The reality is that a woman with a strong sense of independence has a strong sense of self-worth. Hence, she has a healthy sense of self-confidence.

Self-confidence urges women to be bold in their decisions and actions, whether it's starting a business, navigating a business, growing their careers, or sustaining their families. In most cases, women are as confident in their abilities as men. The difference is women don't always express it due to the societal and gender stereotypes that weigh so heavily upon them.

This type of weight results in uncertainly about how we should present ourselves to the world. Unfortunately, this results in a fear of backlash and self-doubt which causes us to suppress the confidence we have deep down inside of us. When we fail to promote ourselves and project our confidence, we hinder our ability to bring our gifts and knowledge to the table.

Many women embrace the subservient narrative as a fact of life and even internalize it so that it becomes characteristic of their personality. However, it's important to distinguish between having a servant heart and a lack of confidence. We should all have a heart for others and seek to serve a greater good beyond ourselves, but we should never belittle ourselves in our efforts to do so. This means, you should never hide or diminish your abilities or your thoughts.

No one else will ever value what you're capable of or what you have to say if you don't embrace it yourself.

Your marital status or "place in society" has nothing to do with the greatness that is inside of you. The fact that you are single, divorced, married, or in a complicated relationship does not define you or your capabilities. Likewise, your position or title at work should not define your self-confidence. For example, whether you're the doctor or the nurse, the patient needs both to perform at a high level of confidence to survive. The success of your place of confidence.

Your place of work is equally dependent upon your self-confidence to achieve success, regardless of your role and responsibilities. Even your children rely on your level of confidence to reinforce their own sense of security.

WHAT IT MEANS TO HAVE SELF-CONFIDENCE

It's important to distinguish between what self-confidence is and what it is not. Self-confidence is defined as one's trust in their own capabilities and powers. It is having a deep trust and faith in what you can do and how you do it. Self-confidence is not a superiority complex. Unfortunately, many of us have been acquainted with the wrong ideology of what self-confidence is which can cause us to dig a hole for ourselves. In as much as you are advised to trust in your own capabilities, it does not make you, your capabilities, or your methods better than anyone else's.

It does not give you a license to lord over other people and emphasize their shortcomings. Your way it not the only way.

You can trust in your capabilities and powers without belittling that of others or making them look inferior. We are all allowed to do things using different methods and by applying our own unique strengths. The way another person exhibits self-confidence may be different from the way you exhibit yours.

Self-confidence is saying, "I believe I can handle this project very well," compared to, "I am the only one who can handle this project, and even if others tried, they couldn't do it like I can", which is self-absorption.

Even if one person's method may be louder and attract more attention, it does not diminish the quiet strength that someone else is exhibiting. It is possible for you to be great and others around you to be great simultaneously.

Now that you're clear on how not to abuse self-confidence, be assured that self-confidence is not self-absorption and does not make you conceited, nor does it make you restrictive with those around you. In fact, confidence is best expressed by accommodation. This can be likened to the way we treat our relationships, personally and professionally.

For example, when we have a high level of confidence, we tend to have higher levels of trust in our partners' actions with or without us being present. When we have a high level of confidence in how we've trained our co-workers and team members, we tend to be more flexible with projects and deadlines. When we have a high level of confidence in how we've raised our children, we tend to give them more freedom with their friends. Self-confidence is most evident when you're confident in your own capabilities, despite that of those around you.

In self-confidence books, you do not have to bring others down to make yourself look better. Of course, there is competition in life, and most times, we are competing with others for the top spot whether we like it or not. But a self-confident person competes fair and square with the belief that what they have is enough to get them what they want. Self-confidence is the best fuel for your self-esteem.

DAMAGED CONFIDENCE

Aside from societal projections, as women, we are greatly influenced by your past experiences—what we were was told, how we were treated, and how we internalize past failures. When your confidence is damaged, it is projected in everything you do in your personal and professional life.

Here are some signs that your confidence might be damaged.

1. Low self-esteem—feeling like you're not worthy of the things you want or the opportunities given to you.

2. Fear of change—being afraid to do anything outside of the norm because it challenges what you already know.

3. Holding back—withholding what you know or how well you can do something for fear of overstepping your boundaries or making others uncomfortable. This is also true for how you present yourself to the world in the way you dress or carry yourself.

4. Feeling threatened by others' success—constantly feeling the need to compete with everyone around you for fear that their success makes you less relevant. This can also be projected in the form of bullying others or putting others down.

TIPS FOR BUILDING SELF-CONFIDENCE

1. **Practice:** The more you practice and prepare for something, the higher your confidence the confidence you have in yourself to perform at your best. Practicing your strengths allows you sharpen your skills and refine them even more. Practicing

areas where you're not as strong gives you confidence in your ability to improve and become better. The more you do it, the better you become at it, and the more confident you are in yourself. Confidence is built one day at a time.

2. **Self-development:** Never stop working on yourself. Just as you should never stop learning, you should never stop growing as a person. The more you get to know about yourself in every area of your life, the more confident you become in who you are. No one else can make you better. Only you can do this. Learn more, push yourself more, gain a better understanding of what makes you tick and how you can become better.

What do you have a low and high tolerance for? What your like and dislikes are? What brings out the worst and best in you? Where do you need to work on yourself so that you are your best self?

3. **Document your achievements:** Keeping track of your achievements makes your progress plain. When you write them down, there is no disputing your accomplishments and what you did to accomplish them. Documenting your achievements also builds your confidence by reminding you of what you're capable of, including your resolve to

overcome barriers. This is especially beneficial during times when you begin to doubt yourself.

4. **Take the lead:** Get comfortable with stepping off the sidelines. Take opportunities to lead projects at work, speak up during meetings, and even organize community and family events or gatherings. You'll never refine your ability to assert yourself and apply your skills with confidence if you don't put it to practice. There's no better way to build confidence than to throw yourself into the water and depend on your own abilities by taking the lead.

Taking the lead requires you to use strategic thinking, apply problem-solving skills, effectively communicate, and mobilize others in a way that boosts your confidence in your own abilities. This also builds your confidence in your ability to effectively mobilize others to achieve a common goal.

THE BENEFITS OF HAVING SELF-CONFIDENCE

1. **It brings peace and calm into your life:** The more your confidence in your abilities, the greater your peace in life. You are less anxious about what will be because you know that you have put your best

foot forward. You don't second-guess yourself about everything you do because you walk in confidence in your abilities. Greater confidence in your abilities reduces your anxiety. For instance, the more confident you are about a presentation for work or a certification, the less anxious you are about it. Confidence provides a sense of assurance that relaxes both you and those you interact with in your personal and professional life.

2. **It motivates and elevates you:** When you're confident, you're motivated to do even more. You feel motivated to expand your horizons and make even more of a difference in your life and the lives of others. Being highly motivated elevates your efforts to achieve your vision. You're more apt to make that career change, start that business, take that trip, start counseling, or take that exam. You have a natural desire to reach higher and be your best possible self.

3. **It builds your resilience:** Confidence increases your ability to persevere. You become more resilient in accomplishing your vision. You operate in the belief that you can overcome anything and that nothing can stop you. You can push through anything. You have what it takes to make the "impossible" possible. You become unstoppable,

bold, and fearless to the point where your light is blinding to your obstacles and enemies.

Shine Your Light: Self-Reflection

Take time to answer the following questions.
1. Are you as confident as you'd like to be? Why or why not?
2. What messages have you been given about women and confidence throughout your life?
3. What are some past experiences that may have negatively impacted your self-confidence? In childhood? In adulthood?
4. Do you ever find yourself crossing over into self-absorption in the place of self-confidence? If so, how?
5. Which of the tips for building self-confidence do you feel you need to practice most and why?

LET YOUR LIGHT SHINE
Becoming the **Best Version** of Yourself

Chapter - 09

WALKING IN YOUR PURPOSE UNAPOLOGETICALLY

"You have to see yourself first".

It is one thing to find your purpose, but it is another to own it. This means walking in your purpose without apologizing for it. Recite the following passage aloud:

- I AM ALL THAT I THINK AM AND MORE.
- I AM CAPABLE.
- I AM COMPLETE.
- I AM RIGHT WHERE I'M SUPPOSED TO BE.
- I HAVE WHAT IT TAKES TO START AND SUSTAIN MY DREAM.
- I AM THE BOSS OF ME.
- I AM THE MAIN CHARACTER OF MY STORY.
- I CALL THE SHOTS IN MY LIFE.
- I AM FABULOUS.
- I AM GORGEOUS.
- I AM FILLED WITH GREATNESS.
- I WILL SHINE MY LIGHT.
- AND I WON'T APOLOGIZE FOR IT.

You know what your purpose is, you're ready to go for it, and you're determined not to let anything get in your way. If you're going to do this, you have to give it 100%, not 50%, or 75%. Even 99.5% won't do. You have to be all in with no apologies or regrets.

1. **Free yourself from the perspectives and opinions of others**. No matter how good your intentions are to go after your dream, until you stop caring about what other people think, say or might do, you will continue to live your life in the bondage of others. The fact is most people don't even care enough to be consumed by your actions and inactions; they're just focused on getting what they want out of life.

Unfortunately, those who do make it a point to dictate what you should and shouldn't do are most often attempting to live (or relive) their lives through you.

Unfortunately, you will likely encounter people who don't want to see you succeed out of jealousy or simply because they lack self-confidence of their own. This is what we refer to as "haters". As nasty as they may seem, they are just confused supporters. The beauty is that haters can't stop your success unless you give them the power to. Don't let the 1% of hate take your focus off the 99% of love.

Of course, there are people who genuinely care about how your actions will impact your future because the want the best for you. And of course, it's appropriate to take their feedback into consideration. But you should always remember that your consideration of others' feedback is just that—feedback that you consider. You should never make the opinions of others the be all, end all. Be careful of how you receive and interpret the constructive criticism you receive. Constructive criticism is meant to be constructive and help you to improve certain areas in your life, not put you off course all together.

Sometimes, we're not afraid of what people have said to us about the life we want to live, we're afraid of what we *think* others might think or say. This is a mirage of thinking that will only hold you back. You wouldn't decide not to take a vacation next year because there's a chance it might rain. Why would you decide not to pursue the vision that's inside of you because of what others might think?

Even if it rained while you were on vacation, that wouldn't stop it from being the vacation of a lifetime. The same is true for what others actually say or do in response to you taking the necessary actions to live out your dream. What people say or think won't actually manifest in your life unless you allow it to.

Remember, you are the author of your own story, which means you ultimately decide what's in it.

2. **Decide what you can and can't live with.** Your life is yours, which means, no matter what others may think or feel about your decisions, you ultimately have to live with the consequences of your decisions, not anyone else. Is your purpose something you can live without? If the answer is no, start living it and stop at nothing to achieve it.

   That career, that business, that relationship you've been putting off—anything that adds meaning and purpose to your life—should be given more weight than the mere thoughts or words of someone else. Can you live with the best *and* worse that can happen in the pursuit of your happiness? If the answer is yes, the decision is clear. It's your life. Decide for yourself what you can and can't live without.

3. **Tune out negativity.** Here's a little secret. Most times, the negative comments that others make about you are actually a reflection of themselves. It's true that 'hurt' people hurt people. People will go out of their way to make your life miserable because they are miserable with their own lives. Sometimes, people are negative simply because they lack the confidence in themselves to pursue their own dream. It's difficult for people like this to see the difficult for people like this to see the positive in

what you're trying to do because they don't have the capacity to conceive dreams of their own, making it almost impossible to conceive of your greatness. When you're approached with constant negativity, don't internalize it. Tune it out and be led by the light that shines within you.

4. **Be true to yourself.** Never try to be anything you're not. Don't try to fit in or be a part of the status quo. Be and do you. You were not meant to be like anyone else, which is why there's only one you. Sometimes, life seems like it's so much easier for everyone else than it feels like it is for you. However, your gifts and character were uniquely designed for your unique vision and destiny.

   Be true to your character and values, be steadfast in your faith, stand up for what you believe in, and let your words and actions be a reflection of you. Start abandoning other people expectations of you so that you can stop abandoning the expectations you set for yourself.

   When you're not yourself, you can't give your all because you live with the weight of falsity. Get rid of the façade so that you can live unapologetically, unrestrained, and free.

Don't compare your purpose or progress to anyone else. This cannot be overstated. You have a unique purpose, and your race is yours, so you run it at your own pace. Our destinies are different, and so are our journeys. Some people might have everything they need on a gold platter while others have to work for it, but the end is still the same. We all have what we need. Comparison is the thief of joy. Don't subject yourself to such robbery. Be content where you are right now but still hunger for the best.

5. **Don't limit your dream**. Many times, we commit to achieving a dream, but we limit how much of it we can achieve, or we diminish it all together because we feel it's too big. No dream is too big. If you're going to pursue your dream, go after it in its entirety. If you don't, the vision that you have for your life will never be realized. It would be like putting together a puzzle but leaving out half the pieces. What good is a half-completed puzzle?

Your vision requires that you achieve all that comes with it, no matter how big, far-reaching, or impossible it may seem. Pursue your passion as though "impossible" doesn't exist. When you eliminate limits or restrictions, the sheer belief in your dream will take you farther than you could ever imagine.

6. Get rid of survivor's remorse. Survivor's remorse (also referred to as survivor's guilt is the painful and guilty belief that one is enjoying the good things in life, such as independence, financial or occupational success, or success in love, while loved ones could or did not. This can be due to someone having died or simply having taken a different path in life. Signs of survivor's guilt include feeling unworthy, confused, or even hesitant about continuing with your success. Survivor's remorse can also cause you to self-blame or become isolated from others.

Don't fall into the trap of feeling guilty for your success because others around you are not successful. It is especially common for women to feel as though they don't deserve their success or that they should hide it because they feel as though close friends or loved ones who they may have shared past struggles and life experiences with should also be where they are.

They begin thinking, thoughts like, "If only I had convinced them to/not to....". This kind of thinking puts an unnecessary weight on your shoulders that is not yours to carry. You are not responsible for anyone's life decisions but your own. And you are most certainly not responsible for the loss of anyone's life. If anything, those who are no longer here with you would be elated about your journey to let your light shine and would be cheering you on right now to keep going!

Shine Your Light: Self-Reflection

Take time to answer the following questions.

1. Do you find yourself making decisions about how you live your life based on others' expectations of you?
2. Are you true to yourself or do you compromise your character to fit in?
3. How good are you at tuning out negativity?
4. Do you dream without limits?
5. Do you feel guilty about your success because of what those who you care about have not achieved (or didn't have the opportunity to achieve)?

LET YOUR LIGHT SHINE
Becoming the **Best Version** of Yourself

Chapter - 10

BECOMING FINANCIALLY EMPOWERED

"Achievement isn't the problem, alignment is. Realign your schedule, realign your priorities, realign your focus".

The wonderful thing about living in your purpose is that it leaves you fulfilled in every area of your life, including your finances. Managing your finances isn't always as easy as it seems. But if you live your life with your purpose in mind, financial freedom becomes much more attainable. If you really want to achieve financial freedom, start walking in your purpose.

Most times, our vision requires funding. the good news is, when you walked in your purpose, what you need to sustain your vision, even financially, will be provided to you. However, you will need to be disciplined enough to manage and sustain your finances so that your vision is also sustained.

Most people struggle to live the life they want for themselves, not because they don't have the means to do so, but because they don't know how to manage the means that they do have, nor do they understand how to plan their wealth. For example, some of the wealthiest people in the world experience bankruptcy because of a lack of money management. You must align your focus and priorities if you want to achieve financial freedom.

FINANCIAL EMPOWERMENT
Financial empowerment is knowing you're in control of your money, rather than your money (or lack thereof) being

in control of you. It's about knowing what you want out of life and establishing a plan to make your money work for you. Financial empowerment can lead you on the path to living your life freely and well. People who feel empowered in their financial lives experience more joy, peace, satisfaction, and pride concerning their finances, and even their success. Financial empowerment boosts your self-confidence and contributes to reduced feelings of stress. The less stress you have, more freely you can live your life.

Just to be clear, money is not the determining factor of success, nor should money be the driving force behind how you live your life. Your purpose should always be at the forefront. It is your purpose that should drive you, not the other way around. It is not uncommon for people to live their lives with the sole purpose of getting rich, only to find themselves miserable in the long run. A truly fulfilling life is one that is meaningful, and a life of meaning often provides for itself, but only if you are intentional with your provisions.

BECOMING FINANCIALLY FREE

1. **Assess your current financial situation.** The first step towards becoming financially empowered is to gain a full understanding of what your financial situation is. What is your income? What debts do you have? How much are you saving? Are your financial habits working for you?

In addition to assessing where you are, take the time to consider where you want to be. Is your goal to purchase a new home? A new business? Growing your business? Whatever your goals are, consider whether your current financial circumstance is where it should be to achieve your goals? If not, determine what changes you need to make and what processes you need to put in place in the area of managing your finances to help you attain your goals.

Set financial goals, budget, and save: When you're financially empowered, you begin to say, "I'm working towards it", rather than, "I can't afford it" because you've established financial goals that you're actively working towards. To do this, you need to ask yourself this question as often as you get paid, "What do I want my money to do for me?" Your money is an agent, and what you spend it on shows what you consider valuable in your life.

What value would you like your money to bring to you? Your answer to this question should inform your financial goals, and your budget should be set it. For example, if your goal is to purchase a home, what financial milestones will you need to achieve? A down payment and the ability to pay the mortgage and insurance are just a few milestones you'll need to achieve. Now that you know what your goals are, you'll need to decide how to budget for them. For example, how much money will you need to include in your monthly budget to achieve your down payment and how long will this take? You'll need to understand your expenses and how much of your income is allocated for your expenses.

You'll also need to be clear on how much you need to save and how much of your income will be allocated to savings. Your savings should be nonnegotiable.

Too often, people consider their savings as optional, and it becomes an afterthought. However, your monthly savings should be given just as much a priority as your rent or house note. Just as you would pay your rent or house note to prevent losing your home, you should pay into your savings as though your future depends on it.

You should also contribute to an emergency fund. This fund is a lot different from your general savings in that it is specifically designed to accommodate emergencies that cannot be planned for. Having a healthy emergency fund prevents you from having to take away from the savings you work so hard to build in the event of an emergency.

The process of setting your financial goals and budgeting is intertwined. Be as detailed as possible when setting your financial goals and rely on your budget as a means to achieve them.

2. **Prioritize needs compared to wants:** Research has proven that the majority of people who earn an income prioritize their wants above their needs. It's natural for us to want to reward ourselves after putting in hard work. In fact, you should. However, rewarding yourself shouldn't come at the expense of your key responsibilities or securing your future.

Becoming financially free requires a high level of discipline and intentionality in your spending. This includes the ability to distinguish between your wants and needs. This might sound straightforward, but people confuse their wants and needs all the time without giving it much thought. Here's an example. You might convince yourself that you "need" to get your nails done every month. However, your nails won't actually contribute to helping you get any closer to the goals you've set for yourself. The truth is, you've convinced yourself that you "need" your nails done when they're actually a "want".

Again, there's nothing wrong with wanting to have your nails done on a monthly basis, but you'll need to decide where they fall in the grand scheme of things. Think of it this way, how much do you spend monthly on getting your nails done (or any other personal indulgence)? Let's pretend it's $50 per month. What need have you been putting off because you "can't afford it"? Would an extra $50 a month make fulfilling that need attainable, or at least get you closer to it? If so, you might want to reprioritize.

If you did this same exercise and identified a minimum of three additional indulgences of the same amount, you could actually free up $150 to put towards your savings or an actual need.

When establishing your budget, make a list of your "wants" vs "needs" and be sure to check it twice. Make a list of wants a need or your savings. Keep in mind that your needs won't always stay the same, which means you should revisit this list often.

3. **Keep track of your expenses and monitor your spending.** You will never become financially empowered if you are not disciplined at tracking what your expenses are and monitoring how much you spend relative to those expenses. Creating a budget without monitoring it would be pointless and won't get you any closer to achieving financial

empowerment. In fact, it can have the opposite effect. If you do the work to establish a budget but fail to monitor, you will only set yourself up for disappointment.

Your budget is an accountability tool. If you don't hold yourself accountable to the budget that you set for yourself, you'll constantly find yourself trying to figure out where your money went and why. This is a cycle that will get you nowhere in terms of achieving your financial goals. It will only set you back and lead you to become increasingly frustrated and less, and less empowered.

Monitoring your budget will also allow you to understand your spending patterns and make necessary adjustments. Make monitoring your budget a part of your monthly (or even weekly) routine. Realizing that you're spending accounting to plan will boost your sense of empowerment.

4. **Spend within your means.** You've likely heard the phrase, "keeping up with the Jones's" as it is often used to describe people's efforts to impress one another through their material possessions. This is the number one reason why we spend outside of our means. It stems from our desire to feel included or be accepted. However, it often leaves us with debt

that even the Jones's can't help us with. Stop comparing yourself to other people and what they have because it will only tempt you to spend unnecessarily. Remain focused on what you're working to achieve so that you don't fall into the trap of spending outside of your means.

Sometimes, we spend outside of our means in because we're actually trying to fill a void. For example, if you grew up without much but you now have a steady paycheck, it might be very tempting to splurge on all the things you never had as a child. Or, if you're having a bad day, you might try to replace your "low" with the high that you get when shopping.

Another reason why you might spend outside of your means is because you're trying to keep everyone else afloat. Always remember, it's ok to help others, but not at the expense of your well-being or your future.

5. **Find a balance between saving and rewarding yourself:** It's important to reward yourself for your hard work, but you should never prioritize constant reward over achieving your financial goals. After all, achieving your financial goals is the ultimate reward because it will provide

you with the financial freedom you seek to live the life you've dreamed for yourself.

The easiest way to find balance between rewarding yourself and saving your money is to budget your reward. Establish a budget for how much you want to reward yourself and how often. This might be a spa day once a quarter or eating out at your favorite restaurant once a month. Being fiscally responsible does not mean depriving yourself of the things you want; it means indulging within your means and obtaining the things you want responsibly.

6. **Pay down debt.** This is a very important part of achieving financial freedom. Paying down debt frees up your money so that it can be contributed to savings and other expenses. Paying down your debt can also increase your credit by improving your debt-to-income ratio. The longer you go without paying your debt, the more debt you'll find yourself in.

This is because most debt comes with interest which accrues over time. For example, if you have a credit card balance of $2,300 for which you only pay the minimum monthly payment of $25, it would take you 13 years to pay off and upwards of $5,000 total, depending on your interest rate. You can reduce this debt by paying more than the minimum allowed balance whenever possible. Don't allow debt to overshadow the plans you have for your future.

7. **Monitor your credit:** Your Credit allows you to received things of value from lenders now, typically in the form of a loan, with the promise that you will pay for it later. When a lender provides you with a loan, it is usually accompanied by interest. The higher your credit, the lower your interest rate.

    Low interest rates mean less debt overtime, which is why you want to keep your credit score high. You can maintain a high credit score by paying your bills on time, keeping a low balance on your credit card (preferably 15% or below), and maintaining open lines of credit for long periods of time to establish credit history.

    Your financial obligations are reported to three main credit bureaus—TransUnion, Equifax, and Experian. Lenders are able to retrieve your credit file from each of these organizations to determine your credit worthiness. You have access to a free annual credit report from all three credit bureaus.

    Additionally, all three bureaus provide free or low-cost credit monitoring tools.

You should monitor your credit on a regular basis to check your progress, avoid credit fraud, and correct errors that might surface on your report. Your credit is in many ways your financial lifeline for major purchases, such as a home, a car, or taking out a business loan. Treat your credit score in the same manner your would the money in your bank account.

8. **Invest.** There are many ways to invest and grow your money for things like retirement and other future goals. If you're working for a company that offers a 401(k), be sure to invest in it, ideally at the maximum level. You can also buy individual stocks and mutual funds using tools such as Robinhood or Stash.

    Investing in real estate allows you to take ownership in assets that appreciate over time, which increases your net worth. Savings bonds and certified deposits (CDs) also allow you to earn interest up until the time it matures.

    This is just the tip of the iceberg when it comes to the number of possibilities for investing. Talk to a financial adviser to help you assess what your investment goals are and determine what types of investments are best suited to fit your individual needs.

Being financially empowered can provide you with financial relief and stability. It also improves your quality of life by allowing you to focus more of your energy on what's important to you. Pace yourself and don't be discouraged by setbacks on your journey to financial freedom. Learn from your mishaps and redirect your fiscal efforts when necessary.

Be steadfast in your efforts to achieve financial freedom. When you achieve one financial goal, it will motivate you to achieve another. Don't expect to get rich overnight, expect gradual results that can benefit you for a lifetime and last for generations to come.

Shine Your Light: Self-Reflection

Take time to answer the following questions.

1. What would being financially free allow you to accomplish?
2. What are your financial goals?
3. Have you established a budget? If so, are you regularly monitoring your expenses and spending?
4. Would you classify most of your reoccurring expenses as "wants" or "needs"? Why?
5. Do you have both, a savings and emergency fund?
6. Are you paying your debt at the rate that you should? What are some things that you can do to reduce your debt?

Is your credit score where you'd like for it to be? What are ways that you can improve your score?

LET YOUR LIGHT SHINE
Becoming the **Best Version** of Yourself

Chapter - 11

BECOMING FREE AND FEARLESS

"You don't have to learn to be more joyous, bring the joy!"

It's time to start living freely and fearlessly, unafraid to take the leap, spread your wings, and shine your light as bright as the sun. It's time to lose the chains that have kept you bound for so long. It's time to lift the weight that you've been carrying that has hindered you from going the distance. You were not made to be caged in or oppressed. Your gifts were not designed to be hidden. Your light is made to shine not flicker.

You are not a prisoner of life, you are the guardian of your life and how well you live it. If you want to become fearless and free, give yourself permission to walk out of your cell. Step out of your comfort zone and create your own joy!

1. **Step out of your comfort zone.** You'll never grow if you only do what's comfortable or familiar to you. Try new things by doing things that you wouldn't normally do. Dare yourself to be bold and push the limit.

2. **Let go of the past.** Stop thinking about what should have or could have been. Appreciate where you are now and get excited about what's ahead of you. You can't go back and change time, but you can determine your future by the way you choose to live your life today.

3. **Learn how to forgive**. Release any grudges or feelings of ill-will that you have for yourself or anyone else. The lack of forgiveness only weighs you down and occupies your thoughts in ways don't allow you to be productive with your time.

   It also robs you of your energy and focus. When you make a conscious decision to forgive those who have created offenses against you (even if it means forgiving yourself), you release negative emotions, such as resentment or revenge.

   When you release toxic emotions such as these, your heart, mind, and spirit become free of the poison that does nothing but cloud your judgement and limit your ability to walk in greatness.

4. **Practice gratitude**. There's no better motivator to live your life freely than to practice gratitude. Having a grateful heart allows you to appreciate your life and all that's in it, including your circumstances and all those around you.

   Think about all the things you've overcome and much better you are because of it. Think about all the positives in your life and how much worse off you could be.

Approach the way you live your life as though you value and appreciate everything about it. When you do this, you become unafraid to embrace life for what it is. You're not afraid to start that business or make that career change. You're not afraid of where that relationship you will take you or to be fully giving of yourself. A grateful heart is filled with love and gratitude. It overpowers hate and fear and creates room for you to live and love even more.

5. **Release control.** You can't control everything. If you live your life trying to, you will only set yourself up for disappointment and add to your anxiety levels. There's only one person who knows the beginning and the end, and that God himself. However, you do have control over your thoughts, your choices, and your actions. What is it that you're trying to control that has you weighed down? Who is it that you're trying to control who won't take initiative for their own lives?

You cannot always control the circumstances around you, but you can control how you handle your circumstances. You can't control what others say and do, but you can control how you respond to them. Liberate yourself by focusing on the things that you can control and releasing the things you have no control over.

6. **Don't be afraid to ask for help**. Get rid of the stigma that comes with asking for help. Asking for help doesn't make you weak or incapable, it makes you human. There is no shame in asking for help when you need it. It is actually a sign that you have a strong sense of self-awareness and that you have the confidence it takes to reach out to someone else for resources or expertise that you might not have.

   The inability to ask for help is a sign of insecurity. If you fail to ask for help when you need it, not only do you hinder your growth, you also risk burning yourself out. Burnout is not an option if you want your light to shine.

7. **Loosen up and have fun**. Give your permission to live a little (responsibly, of course)! Don't take yourself too seriously. It's time to stop watching others live the exciting life that you dream of. Create the joy that you seek! Love, laugh, and live unapologetically, and without holding back. Don't be afraid to be a little silly even. Your life should be as fun as it is meaningful.

   Having fun adds joy to your life, and joy brings your life meaning.

Shine Your Light: Self-Reflection

Take time to answer the following questions.

1. Are you allowing your past to weigh you down? How so?
2. Is there anyone you need to forgive? Is there anything you need to forgive yourself for? If so, what?
3. How has unforgiveness hindered you from living your life freely?
4. What are you most grateful for? How do you express this gratitude in your life?
5. What people or circumstances are you trying to control that cause you added stress?
6. How often do you ask for help when you need it?
7. Do you allow yourself to have fun? If so, how? If not, why?

LET YOUR LIGHT SHINE

Becoming the Best Version of Yourself

Chapter - 12

LET YOUR LIGHT SHINE

"Life is calling to us to give something, not get something".

Once you've found your light, make sure it shines bright for the world and everyone in it to see. What good would the sun be if no one could see it or feel it's warmth? Your light should have the same impact on the world. If you keep it to yourself, your vision and legacy will never be realized. That's because the greatness you have inside of you was meant to be shared.

It's easy to feel as though you can't make a change, but change is made one person at a time. For example, Martin Luther King, Jr. had to have a dream before Vice President Kamala Harris could live hers. Your light can change your circumstances and the world around you.

LETTING YOUR LIGHT SHINE

1. **Give Back:** Helping others is a great source of fulfillment. All the money and fame in the world can't couldn't compare to the fulfillment that comes with giving back to others. As humans, we have a longing to do and see more, no matter how old we get or how much we experience in life.

   Giving back to others is a means for us to do something beyond ourselves and can have lasting effects on the people around us. It's an intangible force that gives us joy and makes us feel complete.

For example, when you give someone a gift, it brings you great joy when you see them actually put it to use or to know that it is meaningful to their lives.

Giving back not only gives us something to live for, it also uplifts others and can positively change their lives. Whether you provide a homeless person with lunch or volunteer in your community, your giving of your time and resources makes a difference in the lives you touch.

2. **Set an example for others:** Another way to let your light shine is to be a shining example to others so that they develop a sense of hope and are inspired to seek the greatness they have within themselves. You can do this by giving of your time and resources, as well as by sharing your knowledge. Be open to giving advice and mentoring others. Be open to sharing your lessons learned so that they don't make the same mistakes along their journey.

Share your accomplishments and help build a support system for those who also desire to achieve success. You can do this formally or informally. For example, you might join a women's club or professional network, or have lunch and share advice with a mentee from time to time.

Don't just "talk the talk", "walk the walk". Live the life that you speak of. There is no better example of success than to see it in action. When you become financially empowered, you leave a blueprint for others for how to become financially empowered. When you become successful, others have a blueprint for how to become successful.

When you live freely, others are inspired to live freely. You can't live anyone else's life for them, but you can certainly inspire them.

3. **Show empathy and humility:** Many people become successful and lose sight of their humble beginnings. They neglect the sufferings of others, forgetting that there too were once where others are in their struggle. Even if you can't relate to someone else's struggle, it's important to empathize with what others are going through. they as well were once there.

Humility allows us to empathize with others in a way that makes them feel human, despite their circumstances, which in turn, gives them hope. The ability to disassociate yourself from pride, arrogance, and even your own ignorance increases your ability to feel the pain of others as if you were the one affected.

It's in your vulnerability that you are really connected with people. Your ability to show empathy with others shines light on even the darkest of places in people's lives. Your words of encouragement or kind actions could be the hope someone needs to keep going.

4. **Maintain a positive attitude:** Everyone loves a person who smiles and spreads joy. In fact, scientific research has proven that smiling is contagious. When a person smiles, neuropeptides, neurotransmitters, dopamine, endorphins, and serotonin are released, which are all chemicals that help lower stress, relax the body, lower heart rate and blood pressure, and even improve mood. Most times, when you smile at others, it is reciprocated because it makes the other person feel relaxed and that it comes from a place of sincerity.

There are very many sincere people in the world, which is why people are very trusting. But you can make it a point to be sincere and show it with your words and actions. Having a positive attitude isn't just about maintaining a smile, it's about exercising patience and handling situations with grace. If you frowned or complained about everything that didn't go your way, no one would ever want to be around you.

In conclusion, as you let your light shine remember to:

- Make it a practice to look for the good in everything, even in people. Make it a practice to see the best in every circumstance so that your mood remains positive.

- Make it a practice to see the best in people and show them that you believe in them so that they have faith in themselves.

- Express joy and hope in your words, your actions, and even in your demeanor.

- Like the sun, your light will warm your heart and the hearts of others.

Shine Your Light: Self-Reflection

Take time to answer the following questions.

1. What are some of your favorite ways to give back?
2. In what ways do you share your knowledge with others?
3. What example are you setting for others in the way that you live your life?
4. How well do you empathize with others? Is your humility what it needs to be?
5. Do you maintain a positive attitude in the best and worst of situations?

LET YOUR LIGHT SHINE
Becoming the Best Version of Yourself

Conclusion

ALLOWING YOUR LIGHT TO SHINE

Our Deepest Fear

By Marianne Williamson

Our deepest fear is not that we are inadequate.

Our deepest fear is that we are powerful beyond measure.
It is our light, not our darkness
That most frightens us.

We ask ourselves
Who am I to be brilliant, gorgeous, talented, fabulous?
Actually, who are you not to be?
You are a child of God.

Your playing small
Does not serve the world.
There's nothing enlightened about shrinking
So that other people won't feel insecure around you.

We are all meant to shine,
As children do.
We were born to make manifest
The glory of God that is within us.

It's not just in some of us;
It's in everyone.

And as we let our own light shine,
We unconsciously give other people permission to do the same.
As we're liberated from our own fear,
Our presence automatically liberates others.

I hope this book has helped you see that allowing your light to shine is what is needed on this Earth. There is a lot of pain and suffering on Earth and you have been a part of it. You know what it is to suffer, to struggle, to be in pain, and to be blinded by feelings of fear.

You life experience has given you a deep understanding of being human and a knowing of how experience is the best teacher and the best way to becoming the best version of yourself.

The good and bad that has happened is part of your journey you're your story. You however, DO NOT HAVE to allow yourself to stay in the company of hurtful people, thoughts and/or experiences
.

Allowing your light to shine means you gather up the courage to change and shift when you need to.

Accept the experiences but step out and become free. Remind yourself of who you are – you are a here to shine your light and your uniqueness. You are a teacher. You have something to share with others, you are unique and have what it takes.

You are free to experience joy and to let go of suffering while doing it.

Now let me ask you this.

- Is there something you've wanted to do for years?
- A yearning to write, or to travel?
- A dream you've held, and yet perhaps abandoned long ago to some dusty shelf in your mind?
- To allow your light to shine you are going to need to learn how to stay FOCUSED. You will need to develop an open mindset to learn new ways of dealing with people, places and new ways of living.

To help shift my mindset and way of living, I found myself leaning on my spirituality and belief. I turned to the Bible and found that find the light, is referenced at the beginning of Matthew 5:16.

It is the inner glow we all possess. It is that positive change within you; that contentment; that inner peacefulness (even when chaos is all around you) that you just can't contain with just being nice or ignoring that it exists).

The light is your understanding that God is your Father, Jesus is your Savior, and your path is being led forward by the loving involvement of the Holy Spirit. It is the awareness that what you were before knowing Jesus personally, and accepting His sacrifice, is nothing like what you are now.

When you let your light shine, you treat yourself and others better, as you understand more and more that God loves you and will provide for all your needs.

This understanding becomes evident to us as the "light" inside you.

Issues that seemed like mountains to scale become more like conquerable foothills when you know God is your guide. Life becomes easier when you know there is a higher power that gives us the strength to take one day at a time one moment at a time.

So, when you let your light shine, it is your way of expressing who you are, whose you are, how your uniqueness matters and how it is all up to you to show up every day, every moment with an openness to allowing your light within to shine.

It is time to allow your light to shine.

So, when life feels too hard and the world feels hopeless, take heart. The best gift you can give everyone around you is your own courage to shine, to help, to rise, to be true to who you want to be, to love the best version of you and living your best life.

Take heart because what's inside is the most powerful force in the universe. Call it light, call it potential, call it whatever feels right to you.

Allow Your light to shine

I look forward to hearing your life journey during Our Women Empowerment Conferences as well as the Bounce Back Empowerment Conference and Workshops. The conferences and workshops are presented both in person and virtual.

As I end let me share a few of my favorite quotes on this topic.

> "Let your light shine today, and let your personality blossom, too. You don't have to be a people-pleaser, just a people-lover." – Beth Moore

> "There are two ways of spreading light: to be the candle or the mirror that reflects it." – Edith Wharton

> "Your work is to discover who you are and then with all your heart give your light to the world." – Jennifer Williamson

> "If you want to give light to others you have to glow yourself." – Thomas S. Monson

"Your only obligation in any lifetime is to be true to yourself." – Richard Bach

"Accept your light and let it shine to create your own lighthouse on a stormy night." – Pauline Duncan-Thrasher

Tell me:
Which of these quotes is your favorite?

You're a light. Remember that. Let that sink into your heart, your life. See what it means, and how it feels, to live into that truth. Other people won't be able to help but notice you.

They will.

DrStem Be Encouraged.

ABOUT THE EMPOWERMENT ACADEMY

The Empowerment Academy is a platform where women can have full access to life, career and business coaching, digital programs, eBooks, and tools for success in life, career and business with membership or individual bookings.

Corporations and Organizations can enjoy providing their employees with state-of-the-art wellness trainings, workshops, and digital programs. Trainings cover mental and health wellness, leaderships -Management skills, mindfulness, time management, organizational skills and more.

The Self-Care Workshops lift women up. The workshops are geared towards letting women know that they can be more, and each workshop provides them with the tools and the support to become more.

The Empowerment Academy provides all round real empowerment: with deep insight programs that address childhood issues, fears, mindfulness, stress management and success programs, with emphasis on an internal and positive change in each woman, so that she can find her passion, and purpose and change her life on her own terms.

ABOUT THE AUTHOR

Dr Stem Sithembile Mahlatini (Life Plus) is an inspiring Coach, Speaker, Trainer and Author. Her passion is Empowering Others through her work as a Motivational Speaker, Author, Coach, Personal and Professional Development Trainer, and Workshop Facilitator. She is also a mindset, and confidence coach for women.

As a Coach, she helps women become crystal clear and successful in their business, work, and life by overcoming fear, self-sabotage, the imposter syndrome, stress, and procrastination.

As a Trainer, her work is focused on wellness, personal and professional development. Some of her popular training includes: Leadership Mindfulness; Compassion Fatigue and Stress Management and The Emotional Toll of the Pandemic-Supporting Your Employee's Mental Health.

Her life goal and mission is to bring HOPE (that is Helping Other People Excel by living stress-free lives, pursuing their purpose and passion.)

Dr. Stem (Sithembile Mahlatini) was born and raised in Zimbabwe, Africa, is the President and Founder of The Annual Bounce Back Better Empowerment Conference, The DrStem Empowerment Academy For Women Risers and Achievers at www.drstemmie.com, The Global Training, Coaching & Consulting Services, Inc, and a certified John Maxwell leadership Trainer.

Dr. Stem (Sithembile Mahlatini) is also an author of over 35 empowerment and inspirational books on her website www.drstemmie.com

Her books are also available on www.amazon.com.

Her Motto: *"We are not given a good life or a bad life. We are given a life. It's up to us to make it good or bad."*
- Devika Fernando

For God has not given us a spirit of fear, but of power, love, and self-control. **2 Timothy 1:7**

CONTACTS- Resources

"Self-Care Workshops Relaxation"
Join Our Memberships to Attend All Our Weekly Workshops For Free or Pay as You Go for each Workshop.

For more information, including workshop topics and dates, visit her website at www.drstemmie.com

One on Once Coaching
For one-on-one Life, Business, Career, Relationship Coaching, please call 781 (254-1602) or email info@drstemmie.com or drstem14@gmail.com for more information.

Digital Courses and E Books
Visit our website www.drstemmie.com and go to **Digital Courses** tab, then the **"Women Empowerment"** tab
https://www.drstemmie.com/empowermentebooks

For Teens, please follow the **"Parent-Teen"** tab:
https://www.drstemmie.com/parentsteensebooks

Bounce Back Better Empowerment Conference
Join us every December for this uplifting, motivating, inspiring, encouraging Virtual Conference until it is safe to meet in person. More info available on our website: www.drstemmie.com

Bounce Back Better Apparel
Visit: https://bouncebackbetterapparel.com/

Women Self-Care Success Store
Visit: https://www.womenselfcaresuccess.com/

DrStem Radio/TV Show & Podcast
Listen on our platform www.InspiredChoices.ca
On Spotify and everywhere you listen to your Podcasts, You Tube, or on Facebook.

Speaker, Trainer
To Book Dr Stem as a Speaker or Wellness, Corporate Trainer please email us at: info@drstemmie.com

Download Corporate Brochure at:
https://www.drstemmie.com/Global-Training-Coaching-&-Consulting-Services-Inc

DrStem Books and eBooks

eBOOKs now available at www.drstemmie.com under **"Empowerment Books"** tab and also available on Etsy www.womenselfcaresuccess.com

These Books are available on **AMAZON** and Book Stores near you.

THERE ARE TWO WOLVES INSIDE EACH OF US

ONE IS EVIL   ## ONE IS GOOD

ANGER · JOY
ENVY · PEACE
SORROW · HOPE
REGRET · SERENITY
GREED · LOVE
ARROGANCE · HUMILITY
SELF-PITY · KINDNESS
GUILT · PATIENCE
RESENTMENT · BENEVOLANCE
INFERIORITY · EMPATHY
DECEPTION · GENEROSITY
FALSE PRIDE · TRUTH
SUPERIORITY · COMPASSION
AND EGO · AND FAITH

Whichever WOLF wins is the one YOU feed most.

DR. STEM SITHEMBILE MAHLATINI

www.drstemmie.com

www.ingramcontent.com/pod-product-compliance
Lightning Source LLC
LaVergne TN
LVHW020429070526
838199LV00004B/328